THE NEW SCIENCE
OF STRATEGY EXECUTION

THE NEW SCIENCE
OF STRATEGY EXECUTION

HOW ESTABLISHED FIRMS BECOME
FAST, SLEEK WEALTH CREATORS

William R. Bigler, Jr.
with Marilyn Norris

Westport, Connecticut
London

Library of Congress Cataloging-in-Publication Data

Bigler, William Randolph, 1950–
   The new science of strategy execution : how established firms become fast, sleek wealth
   creators / William R. Bigler, Jr. with Marilyn Norris.
      p.   cm.
   Includes bibliographical references and index.
   ISBN 1–56720–563–1 (a!k. paper)
      1. Strategic planning.   2. Executive ability.   3. Organizational change.   4. Organizational
   effectiveness.   5. Technological innovations.   6. Corporate profits.   7.
   Corporations—Finance.   I. Norris, Marilyn.   II. Title.
   HD30.28.B545   2004
   658.4′012—dc22   2003057984

British Library Cataloguing in Publication Data is available.

Library of Congress Catalog Card Number: 2003057984
ISBN: 1–56720–563–1

First published in 2004

Praeger Publishers, 88 Post Road West, Westport, CT 06881
An imprint of Greenwood Publishing Group, Inc.
www.praeger.com

Printed in the United States of America

The paper used in this book complies with the
Permanent Paper Standard issued by the National
Information Standards Organization (Z39.48–1984).

10 9 8 7 6 5 4 3 2 1

This book is dedicated to the memory of my wife,

Mary Judith Johnson Bigler,

Who lost a courageous battle with cancer on December 21, 1998,

And to my children Cameron and Taylor, who may learn to love life's journey,
not just its destination.

I hope this book makes a small contribution
to the strengthening of free enterprise.

Contents

Illustrations

FIGURES

TABLES

Preface

In the opening pages of his great book, *The Road Less Traveled*, M. Scott Peck wrote, "Life is difficult." Of course, Peck was writing about our lives as individuals, but I believe the generalization can also be applied to the life of a business. One of the most difficult tasks in most organizations is to execute strategies well. So, I have presumed to paraphrase Peck's words to express the idea that sets the tone for this book: *Strategy execution is difficult.*

The pages that follow contain a combination of approach, methodology, framework, tools, and rules of thumb that address the issues and processes related to strategy execution. The book is my life's work. It is based on many years of consulting and academic work in the field of strategy. And I must recognize here that without Marilyn Norris's collegial input and assistance in editing the text, the book would never have been completed.

This is not a book for light, easy reading. It takes a rigorous approach to what I think is the biggest potential source of value creation in this century—strategy execution. And although much of my experience has been in the world of the university, this is not an academic book. It is designed to be a field manual and roadmap to help executives improve strategy execution in their firms. Our approach assumes that the reader is familiar with the language and tools of strategy and strategic planning, project management, and basic corporate finance. As these topics are adequately covered elsewhere, we focus on bringing a fresh perspective to current thinking and presenting ideas that are totally new.

The book is written primarily for the *Master Builders* in all companies. The Master Builder is the executive who blends together an organization's processes and people to achieve results. My experience in working as a consultant with over 90 firms has shown that the Master Builders are usually the strategically oriented chief financial officers or heads of operating processes and the prime movers, opinion leaders, and cross-functional process teams they lead.

The other senior executives and their direct reports seldom seem to have the primary accountability for world-class strategy execution, as we define it here. Instead, their roles tend to address the accountabilities of the Visionary and the

Architect. The Visionary is the person with the foresight and creativity to intuitively understand the trends underlying changes in customers' buying patterns and to project the impact of those shifts on the business. The Architect, on the other hand, is the one who designs the organization's *form*, including its structure, control systems, and information processes. All three roles are critical to a firm's ongoing success.

Until now, Master Builders have not had a set of guidelines for achieving world-class strategy execution. We hope this book will fill that gap. Much of the current literature on strategy execution seems to address boards of directors who view the company from a 60,000-ft. perspective. Our approach, on the other hand, addresses these issues at ground level—at the "line of sight."

Two recent bestsellers have begun the discussion of strategy execution from a midpoint between the high-level treatment and the "in-the-trenches" approach we present here. In *Execution*, Larry Bossidy and Ram Charan focus on the selection and development of key people and the content and timing of important meetings. In *Good to Great*, Jim Collins, while not addressing execution directly, reports on many strategy execution themes, such as "Confront the Brutal Facts," "Culture of Discipline," and the "Hedgehog Concept."

By contrast, our book offers a dynamic, recurring, process perspective that describes key work in the terms and metrics of executive, operating, and support processes. Only by synchronizing these processes with a given firm's market rhythm is there a chance for achieving world-class strategy execution. We view our book as a complement to the new books mentioned above. Readers may gain from reading *Execution* and *Good to Great* first, and then plugging those ideas into the frameworks of the New Science. Together, the three books indicate a renewed interest in strategy execution as a way of ensuring growth, and they foretell more approaches to come.

A renewed focus on execution tends to automatically synthesize conflicting concepts about the nature of strategy that emerged over the last two or three decades. For example, strategy in the 1970s was a search for an "outlier" competitive position; in the 1980s the emphasis was on favorable positions within an industry structure and on balancing the need to diverge and create breakthroughs with the drive to converge toward a central tendency with little variance. In the early 1990s strategy included the process reengineering revolution and developing industry foresight to discern "white spaces" of latent customer needs.

At the beginning of the new century, strategy began to mean considering the importance of organizational culture in overcoming dogma and inertia and the imperative to revolutionize all aspects of the business model in a search for efficiency and advantage. Today, we think of strategy as the search for new applications of the economics of information as a way of establishing entirely new competitive spaces.

The New Science of Strategy Execution unites these diverse perspectives on two dimensions. One dimension is the process by which adults learn over time to become fully energized in the face of breakneck speed, uncertainty, fatigue, anxiety, frustration, and the tension between personal needs and organizational needs.

The second dimension is an honest understanding of where a firm stands at baseline and finding a way to increase confidence in moving beyond that point. The development of organizational confidence makes strategy execution a key contributor to competitive advantage and value creation.

Creativity, innovation, "strategy as revolution," and white space identification and capture are all possible with the New Science. Following the principles of the New Science instills:

1. A practical appreciation for time—the one nonrenewable resource.

2. A sense of shared destiny in attacking time's common enemies: subject matter, process, structure, and culture barriers.

3. An organic process that extracts the collective resident creativity and innovation in a manner based on a firm's current reality.

4. A platform of success and confidence that quickly improves execution skills.

This book is organized into three parts. Part I consists of Chapters 1–3 and lays the foundation for the New Science of Strategy Execution. Part II contains Chapters 4–8, which detail the five key aspects of the New Science. These chapters build upon each other in modular form so that a firm can begin the process toward world-class strategy execution with the first competency—initiative management—and then pursue additional skills as confidence in execution grows. Part III includes Chapters 9–11 and explores topics such as a program management structure and an overall measurement approach for the New Science. Appendix 4 contains a mini-diagnostic tool that can be used to assess how well a firm is currently executing its key strategic initiatives and to identify the barriers that may get in the way of achieving world-class status.

As strategic initiatives are successfully implemented and cycles of learning are accumulated, the organization's confidence will grow, bigger and bolder initiatives will be put into place, and the full potential of growth in the firm's market value will evolve naturally. This approach has worked for many established firms, and we hope the suggestions provided here will help others to experience the same success.

Acknowledgments

This book is a product of my many years as an academic and a consultant. The ideas I express here owe much to the many professionals I have worked with along the way. I cannot mention everyone by name, but they know who they are, and I thank them all for their counsel, collegiality, and friendship. First, I must say that without Marilyn Norris this book would have never been completed. I have known Marilyn for 17 years and she has once again helped to turn my ponderous writing style into readable text. Drawing on her years in the corporate offices of JCPenney and as editor of *Strategy & Leadership*, a highly respected international journal, she has also contributed greatly to the book's content, and I am proud to have her name associated with its authorship.

Early in my career, I worked in the strategy arm of the Hay Group, which allowed me to learn about the role of human resources and compensation strategy in strategy execution. I sincerely thank Rod Erickson for being mentor, coach, and friend. I had recently left a tenure-track position as assistant professor of strategy at Southern Methodist University, and Rod, Monty Haegele, Jim Hilgren, and Ned Morse helped me make the difficult transition from the logic and language of the academic world to the logic and language of a consultant trying to make a positive difference for clients.

In mid-career, I ran my own strategy consulting endeavor. Here, I was fortunate to work for several public and family-owned, mid-sized companies. In the majority of those firms, I became an ad hoc head of strategy development and execution, which is when the knowledge for this book began to accumulate. Many thanks to CEOs Jody Grant, Rex Jobe, Mike Waterman, Jim Gero, Mike Samis, John Likovich, Ron Gafford, and Albert Black, Jr. They are all brilliant in their own right. For those who knew Mike Waterman, we regret his premature passing in 2001.

During this same period, Charles Phipps of Sevin-Rosen Funds kindly began teaching me about the venture capital industry. And my five-year assignment on the board of the Texas Special Olympics (TSO) allowed me to see first-hand the functioning of high performance teams. Many thanks to all of the fine folks at

TSO, who taught me about the role of heart and for making those the most enjoyable five years of my professional life. Speaking of heart, I would like to thank my longtime associate, friend, and supporter, Bob Edwards—one of the last true gentlemen. His style of counsel is much appreciated.

I spent a brief time with Ernst & Young in Dallas. Serving as a principal in the business-change implementation practice allowed me to understand the role of change management in strategy. Thanks to Daniel Yeast and Bob Ressler for collegial counsel and support. In a similar brief period at EDS, I worked on the company's effort to build a global consulting firm. That experience helped me grasp the role of outsourcing in strategy. While at EDS I also had an opportunity to witness the rich ideas of Gary Hamel and C. K. Prahalad taking shape. My thanks go to John Stempick, John Castle, and Jody Grant for their assistance during a very interesting global startup attempt.

The years I was with the Thomas Group helped to coalesce my thinking as I worked to develop a strategy practice that would complement the group's rich methodology for operating process excellence. Half of the Thomas Group's consulting fees are contingent upon results, which really focused our attention on the execution of initiatives. To work with so many people who were well versed in operating processes literally changed my views about effectiveness in organizations. I owe special thanks to the Thomas Group as they were the genesis of several figures we have cited in the book. Thanks to Jim Dykes, Jim Houlditch, Bill Jackson, Bob Heckman, Ron Johns, Mark Bussey, Pete Cohen, J.R. Smith, John Bridgewater, and Sharon Kimberley. Special thanks to Mark Bussey for some of the exhibits used here and to Bill Jackson, who has become a great mentor, coach, and friend.

My later years at PriceWaterhouseCoopers, when I served as leader for the strategic change practice in the Southwest, allowed me to see the role of strategy in combination with the new economics of information and the implementation of ERP systems in large companies. Both my professional and personal thanks go to Michael Hanley and Steve McClaurin. The way PwC allowed me time with my family during my wife's illness was much appreciated and will never be forgotten. I would also like to thank Greg Silverman (formerly with PwC and now with Design Forum), George Gillen, and Rod Teuber for appreciating and using with clients the first two aspects of the New Science and the mini-diagnostic survey we have included as Appendix 4. The cycles of learning and collegiality of this time are greatly appreciated. Since that time, Greg has been a key colleague, supporter, and contributor to the evolution of key aspects of this book.

From my most recent experience as an outside resource, I would like to thank Rhys Best for teaching me about strategy and strategy execution in a capital intensive industry. His leadership in the face of extreme cyclicality and intense global competition has been remarkable and inspiring.

There have also been some wonderful academic colleagues who have helped shape who I am today: John Slocum, Jeff Kerr, Roy Herberger, Gene Byrne, Mike Ryan, and Ben Kedia, my doctoral advisor. They were invaluable in my professional development. I would like to thank Drs. Bob Lusch and Bill Moncrief of

Texas Christian University in Fort Worth, Texas. Bob Lusch, Dean of the Neeley Business School and Bill Moncrief, Senior Associate Dean, allowed me to be an entrepreneur within the walls of academia as Executive Director of the Charles Tandy American Enterprise Center, where I practiced how to implement executive development and education in a value added manner.

Here, I would like to also sincerely thank my father-in-law, the late Dr. Bill Johnson for help with the concept of environmental carrying capacity (Chapter 7). Bill was a leading genetics pioneer in the poultry science field and our long discussions about environmental attractiveness, carrying capacity, genetic codes, and natural selection were awe inspiring and will never be forgotten. We all miss this wonderful man with a great, dry wit.

In closing, I would like to recognize the influence of my father, Brig. Gen. (Ret.) William R. Bigler, Sr., who taught me the role of hard work, and my mother, Marilyn Genevieve Gautreau Bigler, who taught me how to be empathic and kind-hearted. How my father with austere German ancestry and my mother with gentle roots in France ever got together is a mystery. But their influence has cultivated in me an appreciation for finding a balance between results-oriented hard work and kindness. With her recent passing, we all miss hearing Mother say, "Don't worry, it will all work out." To my brothers, Tom and Mike Bigler, your influence on this book's actual occurrence is more than you know.

Finally, many thanks to John McCarty for his pre-publication support and to Eric Valentine and Hilary Claggett at Quorum Books for seeing the possibility of this project and allowing it to happen. Marilyn and I hope our book will make a small, but important contribution toward helping business leaders improve their strategy execution process and skills, their organizations, their operations, *and* their results.

William R. Bigler, Jr.

PART I

THE NEW SCIENCE OF STRATEGY EXECUTION

Chapter 1

How Established Firms Become Fast, Sleek Wealth Creators

Strategy execution is difficult. Probably no CEO of a company that has been in business for five years or more would disagree. One study has shown that 90 percent of formulated strategies of firms in the United States and Europe are not implemented on time and with the intended results. When Lou Gerstner came on board to turn around IBM, he said execution was the key problem. There was good thinking, according to Gerstner, but initiatives were delayed and shelved, and there was no sense of urgency about hitting market windows. Not long ago, security analysts downgraded Xerox's stock because of execution problems. Two major, unconnected initiatives—back-office automation and a reorganization of the geography-based sales force to a customer-based organization—caused near chaos.

Strategy execution problems usually become even more complex and convoluted than these two examples portray. Today's firms do not seem to depend on general management as a key source of competitive advantage in the global economy. However, we believe it to be the most difficult advantage to imitate. As we propose throughout this book, most strategies go to parity among competitors very quickly. Thus, if strategies themselves cannot provide a clear advantage, then strategy execution must emerge as a critical source of sustainable advantage. In fact, world-class execution has been a perennial challenge. Peter Drucker wrote in 1967 about the effective "execute-ive." His play on the word underscores the view that the key responsibility of being an executive is to execute to results—to go beyond being a thinker and a leader to ensure that strategies produce the intended growth.

Management teams that want to develop world-class strategy execution skills must accept a new strategic paradigm, a paradigm that elevates strategy implementation to a level of importance equal to strategy formulation. In the past, implementation took a back seat to formulation. Good implementation was thought to be simply good project management and/or the right "fit" among strategy, structure, compensation, and culture. The "fitness" school of thought is too static for today's fast market rhythms. And while good project management will always be needed, today's markets require the application of more science and art if the highest expected returns are to be achieved.

STRATEGY DEVELOPMENT HAS CHANGED FOREVER

Six major forces are driving the strategic challenges of the 21st century business environment: globalization, industry convergence, electronic commerce, innovation and growth, disruptive technology, and fading customer loyalty. These forces are causing unprecedented insecurity in strategy formulation. Two additional factors are now contributing to the uncertainty of the situation: shortages of labor in some critical technology competencies and the lasting effects of the tragedy of September 11, 2001. The business climate created by these factors mandates that every strategy be executed with speed, at the lowest cost, and with little or no rework. A wrong play may be scuttled quickly, but at least a cycle of learning can be gained if there are no stalls or rework. Stalls and rework produce very little learning because the ensuing clutter and confusion only serve to obscure an understanding of the root causes and effects of success and failure.

To successfully manage firms and grow their market value in these times, a CEO's strategic capabilities must include eight elements:

- Speed (in everything),

- Executive, operating, and support processes that are synchronized with fast market rhythms,

- Innovation and entrepreneurship,

- Ways to identify and remove subject matter, process, structure, and culture barriers,

- A sense of urgency and a mandate to find and learn from root causes and effects,

- Courage to prudently terminate initiatives,

- Effective grass roots leadership in middle management and above, and

- Results.

To achieve these ends, a very different mindset and approach to strategy execution is needed. First, the notion of time as linear and milestone-based must be replaced with a dynamic and cyclical model. Second, historic barriers that prevent synchronizing processes with market rhythms must be eliminated and outdated processes must be replaced with fewer, faster, sleeker processes. This way of thinking will be revolutionary in most firms, but speedy barrier identification and removal are critical to achieving the key attributes listed above and are the essence of the new paradigm for strategy execution.

Identifying and removing barriers often requires managerial courage. Signaling the need for significant change within long-standing organizations can place limits on the career aspirations of the executives involved. The operating cultures of successful firms are based on constructive executive activism—the willingness to see situations clearly and to take the necessary remedial actions, in spite of the risks. A system of give-and-take much like the free market principles of supply and demand must operate within the firm, allowing all decisions to be based on what is in the long-term best interests of the firm, rather than the short-term best interests of a select group of executives. Successful turnaround actions in firms such as Encyclopedia Britannica and JCPenney demonstrate the value of such activism.

Today's competitive environment brings with it many challenges: moderate to extreme uncertainty, breakneck speed, shorter and shorter windows of opportunity, and more knowledgeable and demanding customers. In addition, firms find they must add new skills, competencies, and technology, seemingly overnight. Meanwhile, important new competitors can spring up out of nowhere, sometimes led by former colleagues who have taken valuable learning with them when they left the firm. As a result, finding a way to excel at executing strategy has become a major source of value creation.

AN OVERVIEW OF THE NEW SCIENCE OF STRATEGY EXECUTION

The New Science of Strategy Execution combines innovative and traditional management practices to make strategy execution the most difficult to imitate source of sustainable competitive advantage. The New Science addresses the importance of a number of operational and strategic factors:

1. Corporate center structure, role, and process.

2. Executive, operating, and support process synchronization with market rhythms.

3. Creative funding sources and resource allocation processes.

4. An organizational culture that allows powerful executives to recognize mistakes gracefully and helps the organization to learn from those mistakes.

5. Measuring strategy execution drivers and results weekly.

6. Quickly identifying and removing subject matter, process, structure, and culture barriers to clear away clutter and confusion.

7. Implementing a key executive process for initiative management with venture capital metrics of speed, yield, and returns.

8. Creative, rolling processes for revenue/cash flow forecasting that eliminate budgeting, annual operating planning procedures, and other cumbersome executive processes.

9. Creating a sense of "shared destiny" among all prime movers of strategy execution, encouraging them to attack the common enemy of long cycle times, too much rework, too many stalls, and an inability to terminate unproductive initiatives in a timely manner.

10. A culture and process to install the appropriate form of variable pay so that the people who help to grow the firm's profits beyond plan can share in those gains.

The selection of the above factors is based on two premises: (1) Adults cannot easily increase their *individual* innovation and creativity potential, no matter how much training and coaching they receive; (2) However, an adequate amount of innovation and creativity to ensure future growth resides *collectively* in the people of most incumbent firms.

The question becomes how to extract these collective ideas in a way that works to create wealth. The answer requires three interrelated processes:

1. Creativity must go through a process to emerge as innovation.

2. Innovation must go through a process to emerge as a priority initiative that has sufficient funding and true commitment.

3. The prioritized initiative(s) must go through a process that allows critical input from all of the executive, operating, and support process owners of the firm; identifies and removes barriers; and applies metrics for assessing cycle time, rework, customer satisfaction and value, cost, and financial return.

These three subprocesses (discussed in detail in Chapter 10) contribute to a new view of strategy execution and provide an exciting execution vehicle to pursue opportunities and generate returns. This execution vehicle has at its foundation an initiative management process that contains applied process and portfolio disciplines, such as:

• Honest assessment of the baseline situation.

• A practical, universally agreed upon method for prioritizing proposed and in-process initiatives.

• A portfolio containing an adequate mix of incremental, support, and breakthrough initiatives for diversification and proper leverage of resources.

• Line balance in the initiative management process so that the portfolio does not create bottlenecks that stall initiatives during the four stages of their development.

• Metrics that encourage the earliest possible termination of an active initiative, thus releasing initiatives from backlog and freeing resources.

• Fast forwarding the likely impact of the initiatives in various stages of the four-stage process on expected increases in the market value of the firm.

• The timely identification and removal of subject matter, process, structure, and culture barriers.

• A leadership imperative that drives each initiative to ultimate financial realization and does not allow stalls or a lack of vigilance at the breakeven point.

The New Science offers strategic insight and execution excellence by:

• Revitalizing management's strategy execution skills by focusing on leadership and the management of initiatives and opportunities.

• Offering a new path to competitive advantage by prioritizing, aligning, linking, and synchronizing executive, operating, and support processes to the rhythms of the firm's marketplace.

- Providing a first-of-a-kind way to measure market rhythm—a tempo based on, but shorter than, the buying cycles of key customers.

- Managing opportunities and initiatives to meet the mandate for continuous growth, and mapping a winning and practical innovation journey.

- Outlining an effective way to schedule, manage, and synchronize key competitive thrusts in line with marketplace realities.

- Providing a new way to picture, map, and manage ripple effects of change on an organization's power bases, processes, functions, and accountabilities.

Many firms have recently invested in projects such as shareholder wealth improvement, process reengineering, growth and innovation, enterprise resource planning (ERP) implementation, and benefits-realization. These firms are ready to leverage those investments immediately by taking powerful steps forward with the New Science of Strategy Execution. Later chapters in this book provide the guidance they need in applying the principles of the New Science.

There are other firms, however, that are not yet ready to deal with 21st century challenges. These firms exhibit one or more signs of dysfunctional strategic management. Principles of the New Science can help these firms to dramatically improve strategy execution by eliminating the causes of their dysfunction.

SYMPTOMS OF ORGANIZATIONAL DYSFUNCTION

Firms that are dealing inappropriately with current challenges exhibit some obvious symptoms. Below is a list of many of the symptoms that have appeared during strategic and operational audits in a number of firms. While some firms exhibit only one or two of these symptoms, other firms may experience them all. The symptoms can foretell serious dysfunction, even though current accounting numbers look good. In fact, many of the firms exhibiting these symptoms are still rated as highly desirable by Wall Street. But, eventually, the dysfunction will dampen their value ranking in the eyes of investors. The symptoms of dysfunction are:

- Unprofitable growth.

- A widespread sense of drifting and being stuck in neutral.

- Key competitors stealing market share while financial numbers are showing misleading good indicators.

- New entrants from other industries stealing market share.

- Moderate to heavy initiative overload confusing effort with results.

- No true commitment to stick to the resource allocations in the strategic plan; stealth initiatives and substitute processes cropping up everywhere.

- Continual suboptimizing caused by pursuing department self-interest at the expense of company goals.

- Historic evidence of inability to implement to timely results.

- Moderate to severe dysfunction in the top management team, for example, infighting, lack of accountability, and finger pointing.

- Arrogance in the culture and inability to challenge dogma.

- Mistaking momentum for strategic leadership.

- Key talent leaving the firm.

- Chronic frustration, fatigue, and free-floating anxiety.

- Systemic decline in employee morale in all units.

- Board of Directors pressuring for change, but unable to offer help.

- Constantly depending on one big home run initiative.

- Prevalence of seemingly drastic, flip-flopping, stop-gap measures.

- Top management team in fire-fighting mode, with tendency to micro-manage, or remaining aloof from operational and support processes.

- Key financial targets missed for more than three consecutive quarters, accompanied by declines in the market value of the firm.

The symptoms signify that the company's executive, operating, and support processes are counteracting or interfering with each other. They are not prioritized, linked, or aligned and are severely out of synchronization with the firm's market rhythm. Growth, innovation, and market-based entrepreneurship have typically taken a back seat to cost cutting, reengineering, and turnaround activities. Often, disparate decrees from a board of directors make timing of the key competitive thrusts inappropriate, thus compounding problems. In addition, piecemeal decisions caused by vertical organizational structures and silo decision making make it difficult to perceive or understand ripple effects in other parts of the organization before it is too late to take remedial action.

CONCLUSION

In this chapter, we have cited many reasons why strategy execution is such a perennial challenge for firms and why it can become a valuable source of competitive advantage.

We conclude here by emphasizing two key pieces of the successful execution puzzle. The first piece is the prevailing notion of time. For most people in the developed nations of the Western world, time is linear and milestones are used to mark progress. Many of today's business managers have been trained in the critical-path method of project management, and as powerful as this tool can be, it can lead into a trap. In the prevailing lore of project management, forces that are deemed beyond human control allow all milestones to slip forward, with little urgency to understand that time and critical learning have been lost and can never be regained. Successful execution demands that time be perceived as a recurring, dynamic process. And while uncontrollable events may cause delay, what can never be compromised is learning about the root causes of these delays so they can be avoided in the future.

In Chapter 5, we see that the strategic work of any firm should be examined as the interrelationships in three types of processes: executive, operating, and support processes. When key initiatives do not hit their intended targets at world-class speed, process metrics can be used to drive a weekly drumbeat and can at least help to gain a cycle of learning. These metrics operate at the level of root causes, not at the level of symptoms. There are five key root-cause metrics: process cycle time, amount of rework, process cost, customer satisfaction, and customer loyalty. Symptom metrics measure things like employee satisfaction, satisfaction with supervisors, and the firm as an employer of choice. While these measures are important, they are really outcomes of improving the root-cause metrics to world-class standards. When time is viewed as linear and milestone-based, there are no recurring process metrics. Instead, symptom metrics are pegged to milestones, which means there can be no real cycles of learning. There may be hypotheses and finger pointing—but no real learning. The time and the potential learning are lost forever.

The second key to successful execution is to reverse the tendency to confuse effort with results. As long as people are applying effort (often truly working very hard), shifting milestones caused by uncontrollable forces allows managers to rationalize that people were doing their best and missed deadlines will be made up later. But trying to recover from missed deadlines almost always introduces "hot lots" into the affected processes and causes further bottlenecks and delays. A hot lot is typically a hurry-up initiative that is launched without concern for its ranking in priority to other initiatives. This kind of initiative can have two very injurious results. First, it soaks up resources from the approved initiatives, and second, because the business case for a hot lot can be faulty, it may stall or require rework.

The chapters that follow contain a complete methodology that can help business executives improve strategy execution, converting it into a unique and renewable source of sustainable competitive advantage.

Chapter 2

The Foundations of the New Science of Strategy Execution

The New Science of Strategy Execution rests on four essential foundations. Three of these foundations are innovative parts of the New Science: measuring a firm's market rhythm, measuring executive process cycle time, and instituting the process of initiative management. The fourth foundation—applying new measures for evaluating executive efficiency, productivity, and effectiveness—recasts traditional methodology in operations and applies it to executive processes.

FOUNDATION 1: MARKET RHYTHMS

Simply put, market rhythm is the true, underlying tempo of the market as determined by the buying patterns of a company's best customers. The rhythm arises out of those customers' latent needs and dissatisfactions in parallel with competitors' efforts to lure them away and compounded by the possibility of added competition from new entrants into the market.

A firm's market rhythm describes the pace at which it faces a competitive challenge as customers decide where to buy the products and services they want or need. As a rule of thumb, a firm's true market rhythm is about four to five times *faster* than the buying cycle of its most important customers. For example, if the 20 percent of a firm's customers who buy 80 percent of its products and services buy every three months, the market rhythm would be every two or three weeks. A high-end U.S. retailer determined that its best customers purchase about once a month, which means that its market rhythm is five or six days. Thus, within that brief window of time a customer could switch from one retailer to another.

The market rhythm rule of four to five times as fast as key customers' buying cycles was derived from research conducted over a two-year period with three Fortune 100 clients. Appendix 1 contains a sample questionnaire that was used in collecting data in that study. While this general rule is a good starting point, the firm must eventually estimate the market rhythm for every major customer group. For many firms, this may not be an easy task. However, without this important insight into the tempo of customers' buying habits, firms can become wealth destroyers or outright failures in achieving their strategic objectives.

Analyzing and understanding market rhythms reinforces the importance of rethinking time from its usual, linear formulation to a more cyclical pattern. Aligning to market rhythms means that the activities of a firm's entire strategy execution system must be mapped against its market rhythm, rather than against some pre-ordained calendar of events. For example, the executive strategic planning process in most companies occurs as a huge spike of activity for a few weeks near the end of one fiscal year or the beginning of the next, with little or nothing happening in the remaining weeks or months. Multiply this example by the other subprocesses in the strategy execution system, and it is easy to see how out of sync with market realities companies on a linear schedule can be. Factoring in the possible mismatch with other executive processes shows the potential chaos that could result from the seeming orderliness of following an annualized calendar of strategic activity.

Figure 2.1 shows these relationships graphically. The executive processes of the firm are usually the most out of sync with market rhythms, but support processes and operating processes can also be out of alignment. This may be surprising, given that many firms have spent time and resources on process reengineering. Their reengineering efforts may have improved process cycle times but failed to prioritize, align, link and synchronize them with market rhythms and new initiatives.

There are a number of risks associated with ignoring the challenge of market rhythms. The most immediate risk is that a key customer could switch to a competitor. If synchronization is completely lost, it opens the door for even greater risk as the market becomes ripe for one or more new entrants to come in and change the rules of the competitive game. Given the realities of the current business environment, it would appear that the risk of not dealing with market rhythms is much too great.

FOUNDATION 2: EXECUTIVE PROCESS CYCLE TIME

Because the executive processes of most firms are likely to be significantly out of alignment with market rhythms, one of the foundations of the New Science of Strategy Execution is to understand executive process cycle time. Cycle time is estimated using a simple but powerful formula:

Cycle Time = Actions in Progress / Processing Speed

The formula works for all processes, but the focus here will be on executive processes. The numerator in the formula, actions in progress, represents the major initiatives that have been derived from strategy development, strategic planning, and operations planning. The denominator of the formula, processing speed, is found by estimating how many major initiatives are active in a typical year and then determining how many major initiatives were completed during the last year.

Figure 2.1
Defining and Measuring Your Market Rhythm

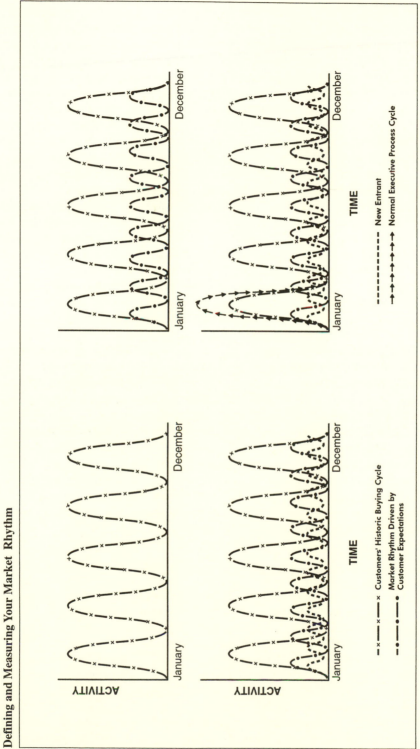

In identifying completed initiatives, two caveats must be observed. First, an initiative is considered to be complete when its last deliverable is finished *as defined in the original business case*. Second, an initiative is early, on time, or late compared to *the date in the original business case*, not an agreed-to slip date. Uncontrollable events may make slippage unavoidable, but rationalizing that an initiative is on time if completed by an agreed-to later date is foolhardy. World-class execution always measures against the original business case, and if an initiative is late, it is late. The root cause of the lateness could be process and culture barriers that can be removed or remedied. However, these barriers may never be identified if teams are allowed to rationalize lateness. These rigorous definitions are critical to understanding executive process cycle time.

When discussing process cycle time, one company executive reported that his company had about 25 major initiatives active in a typical year, and they completed about five. When plugged into the formula, these calculations reveal a five-year cycle time for a major initiative! How can this be? The answer is that we are measuring dynamic cycle time. Over the course of a typical year, new initiatives become active as current ones are completed. The danger is that the numerator—a function of management behavior—may grow too large, too quickly (resulting in classic initiative overload), while the number of completed initiatives—a function of processing speed—falls because of barriers such as stalls, delays, or reassigning resources to newer initiatives. When this situation arises, the cycle time for completing a typical initiative becomes unacceptable.

In assisting the client described above, we examined the best efforts of the company's competitors and found that, if the firm was to remain competitive, the cycle time for initiative completion could be no longer than one year. The company's cycle time had to be reduced by four years! The first step was to reduce the numerator by limiting active initiatives to a critical few. When these initiatives were completed, others could begin. The second step was to increase the denominator, the number of initiatives completed during the year, by removing functional barriers and using technology wherever possible to enable the process. Figure 2.2 illustrates the stages in moving from a baseline situation to the desired levels of cycle time for matching the executive process of initiative management to market rhythms.

FOUNDATION 3: A PORTFOLIO OF INITIATIVES

In the New Science of Strategy Execution, initiatives are the key pieces of work that are expected to directly increase the market value of the firm. Thus, the firm must maintain a portfolio of initiatives with various objectives and in various stages of completion. In order to reduce the cycle time of executive processes as described in Foundation 2, the number of active initiatives must be limited to the few that are of highest priority so that the necessary resources can be made available. This task requires a practical way to prioritize proposed initiatives, ranking in favor of those with an action orientation.

The New Science utilizes an analytic tool called the figure of merit (FOM) in making priority decisions.[1] While there are a number of ways of calculating FOM,

Figure 2.2
Finding the Market Opportunity in Cycle Times

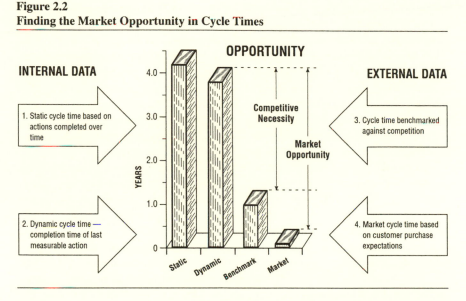

the best approach is one that is simple and begins moving initiatives through the pipeline:

FOM = Expected Cash Benefit of the Initiative / Time to Complete / Cost to Complete

The numerator of the formula consists simply of expected revenue or cash flow. This dollar amount is divided by time to complete and cost to complete. Because there is a universal tendency to keep pet initiatives around too long and to be unwilling to terminate initiatives that received significant prior investment, the formula omits all prior investment. A high-ranking FOM, therefore, requires that an initiative have a high benefit with relatively low time and cost to complete. This automatically orients the initiative management process to action.

This methodology could be viewed as shortsighted because it does not place a high value on critically important strategic initiatives that take a large investment in money and time. This criticism is partly true. The New Science is biased toward action, but experience has shown that an action bias creates more winners. Those who rely on too many big "home-run" initiatives lose more often than they win.

When all initiatives have been rank-ordered using FOM analysis, those that do not qualify for immediate attention become part of a pool of backlogged initiatives. The demarcation between active and backlogged projects is reached when all available resources for the planning cycle have been consumed or assigned. Simply add the completion costs and draw a line at the cut off point. Those above the line are active and are to be put into play. Those that are backlogged can become active only when an active initiative is completed or terminated, thus releasing resources.

A feature called "strategic override" provides an exception to the FOM ranking process. This option allows a firm's executive team to fund an initiative that may have a lower FOM if it represents a prior commitment to customers or is a previously funded, crucial piece of a more complex strategy.

In addition to prioritizing the initiatives, it is important to categorize them in relation to others in the entire portfolio. This categorization uses several lenses, but in sum it describes the initial vision, mission, strategy, and business case of the initiative. Potential categories include: (1) Type of growth: getting better (incremental growth), getting broader/bigger (platform growth), or getting bolder (breakthrough growth); (2) Proposed outcome: revenue growth, strategic initiative, whole business generation, or support initiative; (3) Impact on shareholder wealth: low, moderate, or high impact expectations.

Having a simple scheme of categorizing the initiatives helps everyone to focus on the original intent. Changing this intent should be a major decision. When personal egos become involved in an initiative's journey, its specifications can be inappropriately changed, costs can escalate, and the initiative can be delayed in reaching the market. Sometimes it is better to terminate the project and start again with a new team and new initiative rather than change the intent midcourse. The initiative management process elevates these issues to the level of a senior management team. Without this attention, they could easily be addressed in a piecemeal, suboptimal approach.

At any given period of time, the contents of a portfolio of initiatives should be categorized as active or backlogged and according to one of the three dimensions of strategic intent listed above. It is important to balance the active and backlogged initiatives across all three dimensions. A concentration in one area could be a sign that there is not enough diversification in the portfolio and that "all the eggs are being put into one basket."

This process is important for two reasons. First, it establishes the original, intended vision, mission, and strategy of the initiative and communicates these intentions clearly. Second, it facilitates efficient communication among the people who are involved in the initiative management process. Although these category dimensions tend to be somewhat internally related, that is, a revenue growth initiative will usually be incremental in nature and expected to have moderate impact on shareholder wealth, creative variations can always occur.

FOUNDATION 4: NEW MEASURES FOR EXECUTIVE EFFICIENCY, PRODUCTIVITY, AND EFFECTIVENESS

The final foundation piece in the New Science of Strategy Execution is a way of taking measures of efficiency, productivity, and effectiveness usually found in manufacturing and operations and recasting them in relation to executive processes. Our diagnostic work with clients indicates that executives in senior and middle management must improve their productivity, efficiency, and effectiveness at least threefold.

While productivity, efficiency, and effectiveness may seem like very mundane factors, they offer practical solutions to strategic success. Far from being mundane, these concepts can be translated from the shop floor to the executive suite in ways that are fresh, exciting, and valuable. In fact, when properly defined, these factors are often found to be more than symptoms of dysfunction; they are among the root causes. The New Science defines the terms as follows:

- Executive efficiency is the speed at which key initiatives are turned into outputs and results with no rework, as compared to the speed of a major new entrant in the industry. Applying the threefold rule would mean that a five-year initiative cycle time must be condensed to 1.7 years; a one-year cycle must be shortened to four months.

- Executive productivity is the percentage of initiatives that hit their original performance targets with no rework as compared to the achievement of world-class venture capital firms. Applying the threefold rule would mean that target hits of 10 percent must improve to 30 percent; a 20 percent success rate must become 60 percent.

- Executive effectiveness is the growth rate of the market value of the firm compared to the market value growth of a successful new entrant. Applying the threefold rule would mean that growth of 3 percent per year must improve to 9 percent per year; growth of 5 percent per year must be boosted to 15 percent per year.

These definitions are designed to value three important facets of the New Science: initiatives, speed, and being right more times than wrong. They emphasize first the drivers of results (speed and yield), then the results themselves. They focus on the barriers that could get in the way and how quickly these barriers must be removed. And, finally, they support the basic forces of entrepreneurship and wealth creation.

The definitions do not address the specific symptoms of dysfunction that were described in Chapter 1. Those symptoms tend to take care of themselves when people work in a system of executive, operating, and support processes that are synchronized to the firm's market rhythm and measured against executive efficiency, productivity, and effectiveness as defined here.

CONCLUSION

We conclude this chapter with a look at a real-life example, although the company will not be named. The company was producing medical imaging products in the United States, but its sales and stock price were falling. At the time of the analysis, the company's cycle time for developing new products was seven to ten years, and the FDA had denied approval for its last four products. The company was forced to buy excess capacity and re-package products from its competitors to maintain sales. Lower margins and the decline in sales caused by the delay resulted in a 50 percent drop in the firm's stock price. Thinking the root cause of the problem was the productivity of its chemical engineers, the company commissioned a very expensive study. The study took a year to complete and yielded unsatisfactory results. Then a team led by the author conducted an analysis based on the four foundations of the New Science as described here. The true root causes were revealed in only three weeks. Here's what we found.

1. A convoluted and highly informal suite of executive processes was short-circuiting the firm's efforts in strategic management and denying R&D and new product development the necessary commitment for staying the course. Pet projects were launched frequently, causing hot lot bottlenecks. A simple assessment of the dynamic cycle-time formula showed that the numerator (actions in process) was too large and the denominator (processing speed) was too small.

2. Company executives were brooding over the constraints of their seven- to ten-year new product development cycle time instead of focusing on the company's customer-driven market rhythm. Their key customers bought about once a year, creating a market rhythm of about three months!! This is the tempo that should have set the pace for all internal processes. Had the executives developed a "drumbeat" discipline and vigilance around this marketplace reality, they would have been able to focus on the causes of slow development. They would also have seen the need to expand their strategy to include aspects such as service and alliances to maintain customer loyalty and mitigate the stranglehold of their lengthy new product cycle times.

3. The company was depending on four "home run" initiatives rather than having a carefully planned mix of incremental, breakthrough, and new business initiatives. As we see in Chapter 4, such a mix must be led and managed through a visible, overarching process.

4. And, finally, the company's executive team had no measures by which to evaluate and discipline its own executive processes. Applying measures of process efficiency, productivity, and effectiveness and comparing the company's baseline situation with world-class standards quickly showed that the root cause of much of the delay in cycle time was coming from the executive office, not from operating processes. In fact, as a rule of thumb, if all three of these measures are below world-class benchmarks, the root cause of over-long cycle times is almost always in the executive office.

Because of the great importance of initiative management in the New Science, we devote Chapter 4 to exploring this process in detail.

In the next chapter, we discuss the concept and reality of market rhythms and why they are crucial for understanding and implementing the New Science of Strategy Execution. We also introduce our 10-S model, which updates McKinsey's 7 S's from the 1980s. The model provides a touchstone that can remind business leaders of the key requirements that must be managed simultaneously if the firm is to be successful in the competitive environment of the 21st century.

NOTE

1. Brian Twiss, *Managing Technological Innovation*, 2nd ed. (London: Longman, 1980).

Chapter 3

Market Rhythms and the 10 S's of the New Economy

The New Science of Strategy Execution replaces a *calendar-driven* view of execution that is based on a set of events with a *dynamic, recurring-process* view in which synchronization with the competitive environment is paramount. For the purpose of strategy execution, measuring the environment in terms of true market rhythm is key.

MEASURING MARKET RHYTHM

Market rhythm is the underlying pulse or beat of the market. This rhythm is created by a combination of your customers' latent needs and dissatisfactions, your competitors' efforts to attract your customers, and the threat of new entrants into the marketplace. These factors contribute to the unpredictability in the customers' buying patterns. Through research and experience, we have been able to estimate that a firm's true market rhythm is four to five times faster than the buying cycle of its most important customers. For example, if your best customers buy every three months, your market rhythm would be every two to three weeks.

World-class strategy execution demands that key executive, operating, and support processes be synchronized to this market rhythm. Two key processes are especially important here. The first is an initiative management process that produces winning initiatives at a speed of about two to six times the market rhythm time. (This process is discussed in depth in Chapter 4.) For a high-end retailer with a market rhythm of five or six days, a winning initiative must be implemented every 10 to 30 days. This process ensures that a steady flow of "bets" and "options" is timed to coincide with the demands of the market rhythm. Second, critical cross-process information must be available to decision makers in market rhythm time. For the high-end retailer, critical process information from strategic planning, merchandising, store replenishment, outbound logistics, and budgeting were bundled for cross impact and delivered to decision makers at market rhythm frequency. For many firms, information reporting is still calendar-driven —monthly, quarterly, yearly. Even firms that have installed major ERP (enterprise resource planning) systems find that process information may still be out of sync with market rhythms.

Market rhythm capture refers to the number of market rhythms in a given time period in which a company captures the largest share of the economic profit available in each of its product or service segments. Capturing market rhythms can come about in a number of ways. First, customers may find high quality in using the products, and they may be willing to reward the firm for this quality by paying premium prices. Or, the firm may be first to market or a close follower and enjoy price premiums by capturing profitable, early-adopter customers. Costs may be low, or the firm may have a customer service skill that allows it to retain more loyal, profitable customers. In one of the most creative strategic planning formats we have seen, a large European liquor distiller (maker of a variety of popular liquor brands) targets end-consumer "need states" for liquor consumption, such as to "unwind," to enjoy fine dining, and to "cut loose." The firm measures how much of the economic profit pool it captures in each geographic region for each of five major need states. This firm is trying to enhance its strategy execution skill to capture more economic profit more frequently, hence achieving more market rhythm capture.

Market rhythm capture is a key variable in determining what world-class strategy execution can accomplish. The strategy execution grid shown in Figure 3.1 contains a new way of estimating customer value and plots it against unit cost per number of market rhythms captured.

The vertical axis in the diagram is labeled Relative Non-Price/Non-First-to-Market Customer Value. This measure is unusual because it measures the value customers receive from the *pure functionality and quality in use* of the products and services they buy. The calibration points of minus (–), zero (0), and plus (+) indicate the firm's standing relative to its strongest competitors.

Company executives must ask themselves: Do our customers receive more, the same, or less functional value from our products and services as compared to those our competitors offer? When our customers use our products and services, do they perceive them as being of better, the same, or lesser quality than competing products and services? The answers to these questions define the company's position on the vertical axis.

There are two reasons why analyzing value in this way stresses pure customer value without the effects of price reduction and being first to market. First, when prices are lowered, customers may perceive a transitory perception of value, but in time, the lower price becomes the "true" price and a downward pricing spiral ensues. Likewise, being first to market can give customers perceived value, especially in business-to-business markets where customers may have a strategic need to buy first as part of their own strategy. In other situations, being the first to buy may be accompanied by the vicarious excitement of being first. This temporary advantage, however, can mask later dissatisfaction if true quality in use is lacking. What does last, regardless of these changing tactics, is the real, quality-in-use value—and that is what any customer ultimately wants.

Figure 3.1
Strategy Execution Grid

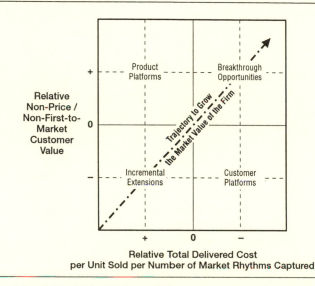

Relative Total Delivered Cost
per Unit Sold per Number of Market Rhythms Captured

Source: Adapted from Michael E. Porter, "What Is Strategy?" *Harvard Business Review* 74, no. 6 (November–December 1996): 62.

Thus, the vertical axis of the Strategy Execution Grid indicates a measure of the pure value the customers receive from using the products and services they buy, while factoring out the confounding effects of price reduction and first-to-market value. The ability to provide superior, pure, quality-in-use value over sustained time periods is one of the critical dimensions in growing the firm's market value.

The horizontal axis on the grid in Figure 3.1 is labeled Relative Total Delivered Cost per Unit Sold per Number of Market Rhythms Captured. The cost measure accounts for all costs in the value chain through to the customer and may include customer service costs as well.

Strategy execution enters the framework in the measure of market rhythms captured. This measure is a better way to accommodate the issues of price and being first to market. On this axis, the relative calibration is reversed for favorableness. That is, when total cost, divided by number of units sold, and then divided by market rhythms captured is higher than that of the best competitor, costs are too high, not enough units are being sold, and/or not enough market rhythms are being captured.

Notice what happens with the math in the analysis on the horizontal axis. Dividing anything by zero equals zero; thus, without market rhythm capture, the market value of the firm will not grow, regardless of how low the total cost per unit sold is or how much quality-in-use value customers receive. Market rhythm capture only happens with world-class strategy execution skill. Formulation is still important, but relying on the brilliance of a formulated strategy alone is too static for today's challenges.

The two axes in Figure 3.1 can be used to diagnose a firm's strategy execution skill at baseline and to identify the quadrant in which it currently operates. The lower left quadrant is the foundation quadrant. In this quadrant, resources are reallocated among processes and capacities for incremental product extensions or to take advantage of quick, top-line growth opportunities. These skills are basic to successful strategy execution.

In the upper left quadrant, the firm leverages competencies for development and execution in major product families in order to maintain or enhance customer value. In the lower right quadrant, the strategy includes serving multiple customer groups with the same competency, capability, and resource structure. Finally, the upper right quadrant represents breakthrough opportunities—changing the rules of the competitive game regarding customer value, cost, and market rhythm capture. Microsoft has enjoyed executing in this quadrant for many years.

Wherever a firm is at baseline, that is, at the point of its initial evaluation on this grid, a growth/innovation path aligned to increasing strategy execution skill and confidence must be laid out. If the market value of the firm is to grow, the path must move from the lower left quadrant to the upper right (see Figure 3.2). This creates a dynamic, action mandate for "execute-ive" teams. The concentric curves superimposed over the quadrants are called "isocurves." At one point in time, a given curve represents a mixture of the elements that label the two axes. That is, at any given time, products and services provide customers with an appropriate mix of value and cost. Higher customer value usually means higher cost and vice versa. The job of strategy execution is to move through a series of isocurves faster or better than competition does. Each time a company moves to a higher isocurve, it establishes new rules of the game for customer value and cost and allows for the greatest possibility of more market rhythm capture.

Once a company has completed the above analysis, it is ready to move to successively higher sustainable competitive advantage by developing increasingly greater skill at strategy execution. This entails five conditions with accompanying skills that form the key aspects of the New Science. These aspects are independent and can be added one at a time as the firm gains in execution excellence. Part II of this book is devoted to these aspects, but we describe them briefly here.

1. *Implementing a process approach to initiative management.* Initiative management is a process that identifies incremental and breakthrough initiatives, prioritizes them for action, allocates resources, puts them into play, and then manages them to the ultimate planned financial return or terminates them quickly if they fail to meet significant metrics for success. Many firms have such a hodgepodge of current, stalled, "stealth," and recently terminated initiatives that their growth efforts are in total confusion. Projects being worked on may be entirely divorced from actions that should be pursued according to a company's vision statement and strategy direction.

   Firms also tend to confuse effort with results. Their hodgepodge of initiatives gives them the illusion that the right things are being done. But while they certainly may be working hard, their efforts only increase cycle times, rework, and cost—the opposite of what is needed for world-class strategy execution.

Figure 3.2
Strategy Execution Grid with Isocurves

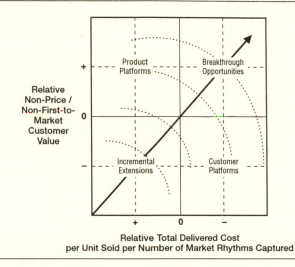

Relative
Non-Price /
Non-First-to-
Market
Customer
Value

Product Platforms

Breakthrough Opportunities

Incremental Extensions

Customer Platforms

Relative Total Delivered Cost
per Unit Sold per Number of Market Rhythms Captured

Source: Adapted from Michael E. Porter, "What Is Strategy?" *Harvard Business Review* 74, no. 6 (November–December 1996): 62.

2. *Making all executive, operating, and support processes prioritized, aligned, linked, and synchronized (PALS) with market rhythms.* Many firms are badly out of synchronization with their market rhythms. They are misled by the seeming orderliness of calendar-driven events, and are unaware of the continuing pressure for innovation that accompanies the market rhythms.

This lack of synchronization is especially evident with executive processes (visioning, strategic planning, budgeting, resource allocation, technology planning, and performance management processes). A large lighting manufacturer took on average 4.2 years to attack any major new lighting opportunity. By benchmarking the best performance of its two major competitors and many of the smaller, more nimble competitors, response time of world-class status was estimated to be 14 months. The company's market rhythm was calculated to be about three months, and when the key measures of executive, operating, and support processes were calibrated, the average cycle time was six months with a first-pass yield of only 40 percent—that is, 60 percent of the output of the processes had to be reworked. The delaying culprit was a group of some 20 executive and operating processes that were not prioritized, aligned, linked, or synchronized with each other, or with market rhythms. Improving and aligning these cycle times paved the way to closing the competitive gap.

3. *Managing all key initiatives against a growth and innovation map.* Once a baseline position on the Strategy Execution Grid is established, a growth/innovation journey must be mapped out. Even though there may be pauses along the way, the portfolio of initiatives must be identified and accountably managed if the company is to meet the ever-present

demand for growth and innovation. Moving accountability down into the organization is an important element in this process if true growth is to be accomplished. The average tenure of a CEO and his or her direct reports is about three years. And because of the lead and lag effects of strategic decisions and eventual results, some executives may be tempted to manage for self-interest, or even mismanage, in the short term. They count on being promoted out of the assignment before ill effects happen, leaving a successor to take the blame. Instilling accountability further down in the organization helps to ensure that initiatives will continue to completion.

4. *Measuring the competitive environment to time-phase four key strategic thrusts: plans for growth, process reengineering, cost reduction, and turnaround efforts.* Inappropriate timing of these competitive thrusts can derail world-class strategy execution. Trying to force-fit a competitive thrust into an inhospitable competitive environment is a formula for headache at the least, outright disaster at the worst. There seems to be a common tendency for an incoming CEO to force a "canned" pattern of improvement—a process that perhaps had worked well in the CEO's former company—into an entirely different situation in the new firm. This strategy seldom works. Publicly reported instances of such miscalculations include: Archie McCardell's success at Xerox, but not at International Harvester; and Gil Amelio's success at National Semiconductor, but not at Apple Computer. While other factors were often involved, the pitfall of trying to do "what worked before" was also operating.

5. *Gaining an early warning of ripple effects.* We know that a key decision in one area of the firm, whether in a process, function, geographic subdivision, or headquarters, can and will cause ripple effects elsewhere. This is a law of organizational life for at least two reasons:

- First, customers are demanding more complex linkages among products, services, and information, requiring more cross-unit and cross-process integration. As companies become "cross-wired," they create a conduit for ripple effects.

- Second, the drive for power is human nature, and it occurs in predictable patterns at the impetus of a key change event. The reality of power in organizations—striving for it, fighting against it, building "fences" to protect it—can cause explosions or implosions within a company and create "noise" and aggravation in the predictability of ripple movements.

Even a small ripple in one place in the organization can have huge consequences elsewhere. Many times these secondary effects are not planned for or anticipated, because there is a mistaken belief that the consequences of a decision will stay within the boundaries of the designated department or business unit. But the mandate for little or no rework within an environment of fast market rhythms means finding a way to anticipate these ripple effects through early warning signals.

The New Science of Strategy Execution offers a way to map and predict macro-burst and micro-burst changes through 11 interconnected modules of activity that describe a company's internal and external environment. Tracing the ripples is possible because there is a predictable order to shifts within the power, accountability, and decision-making processes of a firm.

The mandate for speed, sleekness, and little or no rework also means borrowing and copying quickly from all parts of a firm's extended environment. It makes no sense to reinvent initiatives and strategies if existing ones are appropriate for the job at hand. This requirement should help to make firms more outward looking, but it will also expose them to additional ripple effects from external communities of suppliers, competitors, and alliances. In Chapter 8 we explore the phenomenon of ripple effects more completely.

THE 10 S's OF THE NEW ECONOMY

The points we have discussed so far can be summarized within a framework of 10 S's, which represent the strategy execution requirements in the business environment at the beginning of the 21st century. (This 10-S concept updates McKinsey's familiar 7-S model of the 1980s.) Figure 3.3 depicts the 10 S's in a pattern that shows how they are interrelated for maximum synergy.

Figure 3.3
Ten S's of the New Economy

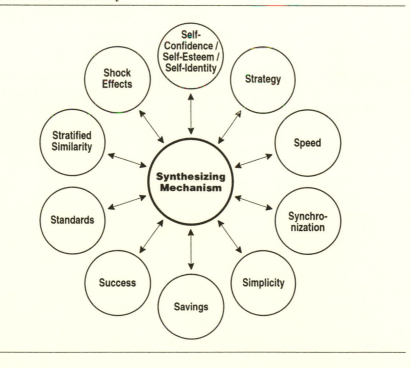

The 10-S model offers a convenient reminder regarding the following competitive requirements.

1. *Strategy.* The shape of the strategy must fit with customer needs and must be a better offer than the competition has made. Strategy shape can be embodied in speed, services,

quality, cost, or innovation. The remaining nine S's help strategy to be continuously adjusted for competitive advantage, growth, and innovation.

2. *Speed.* Quickness and agility are mandatory in everything from decision making to deal making, from planning to leadership, and from on-time delivery to implementation.

3. *Synchronization.* The strategy and speed must be synchronized with accelerating market rhythms and latent consumer needs, and everything the firm does must be in continuous alignment with these rhythms.

4. *Simplicity.* Individual solutions for problems or opportunities need to be as simple as possible. The other S's help to blend simple individual solutions into a modular but united complexity that is difficult for competitors to copy.

5. *Savings.* This S refers to having "high yields" everywhere: little or no rework in all executive, operating, and support processes, being prudent with resource allocation for resource leverage, and continuous, strategic cost reduction.

6. *Success.* Results. Results must be gained or the firm's stakeholders will lose confidence and critical resources may not be forthcoming in the amount and timing required for sustained winning. Both *lead* measures (drivers) and *lag* measures (outcomes) must be optimized in the short-, mid-, and long-term. A proactive communication strategy to investors must be established to continuously "tell the company's story."

7. *Standards.* How good is good? How much is better? How great is great? Standards must be set starting at a company's baseline situation. Simple improvement from last year may be the only prudent standard for the current time period. As success, learning, and confidence continue, becoming the defining entity of the industry may be achievable and necessary.

8. *Stratified Similarity.* This S refers to the fact that much of the energy and structure in an organization is found in similar form (but differing degrees) in many places and levels. In addition, this energy and structure will copy itself easily and seamlessly if barriers do not get in the way. In biology, the cell is "self-similar" to a person, who is self-similar to a small group of people, which is self-similar to a nation, which is self-similar to the universe. A solution at one level can be applied naturally and easily at lower or higher levels. This S is required for quick leverage of knowledge, solutions, leadership, resources, and intellectual capital to achieve competitive advantage.

9. *Shock Effects.* A law of human interaction says that a change in one place *will* (not may) have ripple effects in other places, many times unforeseen. In addition, a seemingly small and unimportant change in one place can produce huge effects in other places. The company must install a model that can provide an early warning of these ripple effects. We provide such a model in Chapter 8.

10. *Self-Confidence/Self-Esteem/Self-Identity.* If the previous S's are accomplished well, the people of a company almost always proceed in their daily affairs with required self-confidence and self-esteem. They will also have a well-defined self-identity, understanding who they are within the company and what value-added role they fill. These feelings of competence are a necessary condition for independent right action in the face

of tenacious competitors and the breakneck pace of today's world. In this kind of environment, policies and rules are largely ineffective in guiding individual right action, since what is "right" changes frequently.

The 10 S's serve as both a launching pad and an umbrella for the five key aspects of the New Science: initiative management, aligning and synchronizing executive processes to market rhythms, mapping the innovation journey, understanding the constraints and opportunities in competition, and managing the ripple effects and interdependencies of initiatives (see Figure 3.4). For world-class strategy execution, all five aspects must operate simultaneously.

Figure 3.4
The 10 S's Launch the Five Key Aspects of the New Science

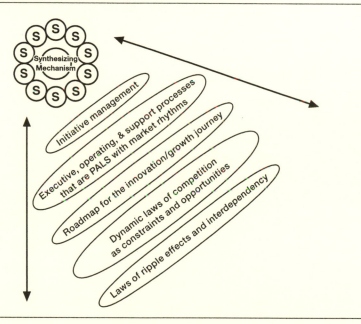

Initiative teams that manage projects related to the five New Science aspects must stay in touch with the 10 S's to ensure alignment, linking, and synchronization. They must provide a system of continuous checks and balances that involves all parts of the strategy execution process. If an initiative, decision, or plan does not align with *all* 10 S's, it is up to the managing team to justify the violation of this requirement.

CONCLUSION

The next five chapters begin the second phase of this book and are presented in the order in which they should be added to the firm's competencies as it seeks to achieve complete world-class capability in strategy execution. Each chapter explores one of the five key aspects of the New Science. While all five aspects are ultimately required, the individual elements are modular and can be implemented as the firm builds confidence through cycles of learning. The initiative management process, which is discussed in the next chapter, can help a firm gain about 40 percent of the required world-class capability.

PART II

THE FIVE KEY ASPECTS OF THE NEW SCIENCE

Chapter 4

Initiative Management for Growth and Innovation

Initiative management is a relatively new methodology. It evolves naturally out of good process management and sets the stage for leveraging previous investments in redesigning and refining business processes. Without a doubt, initiative management is the underlying foundation for world-class strategy execution. This chapter defines the concept of initiative management and explains how it works and what its benefits are. At this time we do not discuss where new initiatives come from in the first place, because we assume that a firm's strategic planning and resource allocation processes are adequate to surfacing the right initiatives. Our focus here is on managing approved initiatives for intended results.

INITIATIVE MANAGEMENT DEFINED

Every strategic planning process includes a calendar of events and a set of initiatives that are approved and funded. These initiatives are typically process-related, functional, geographic, and/or technological in nature and are the key actions that operationalize the company's vision, mission, and strategic objectives. *In the New Science of Strategy Execution, initiatives are the key pieces of work that are expected to directly increase the market value of the firm.* True initiatives are not maintenance, day-to-day activities. While maintenance is as important as initiative work, we believe it is critical to raise the visibility of initiatives that are expected to increase the firm's market value and the barriers that may prevent them from being successful. Completed initiatives, as we define them, will transfer to maintenance status upon conclusion. Thus, initiative management and maintenance become equal partners in business growth. There is definitely no attempt to create two cultures—one the "swift, rich thoroughbreds" (initiative management) and the other the "pack mules" (maintenance operations)—as described by an executive whose organization had a severely dysfunctional management system.

Every year (or in every planning cycle) new initiatives are approved, while active initiatives from previous planning cycles are still in various stages of process and completion. As long as functional, geographic, and process performance are satisfactory, corporate executives can assume that initiative management is being handled satisfactorily. Right? Not necessarily. Functional, geographic, and process performance can often hide problems in the way initiatives are managed. The following case study is a powerful example of how things can go wrong.

DYSFUNCTIONAL INITIATIVE MANAGEMENT: A CASE STUDY

In company XYZ, previously approved initiatives were sometimes inappropriately stalled or shelved. Executives from the business units came together for three days in February for the annual rite of strategic planning. They agreed on the importance of the 15 key initiatives that emerged. "Prime movers" were assigned, and a high-level action plan was generated. But this exercise was meaningless because the initiatives focused on *corporate* change, and the objectives were only indirectly related to the needs of individual business units. As a result, SBU leaders went back to their units and worked on what *they* thought was important. "Stealth initiatives" and substitute processes were launched, using monies from the budgets of the approved initiatives and from unit "slush funds." Because the original 15 initiatives did not have powerful owners and the corporate center was distant and ineffective, these stealth initiatives and substitute processes operated hidden and undetected.

The unauthorized actions helped the SBUs to hit their current year's performance objectives, so company executives believed their management of initiatives was in good order. However, they lost an entire year of improving the strategic and competitive position that the original initiatives were approved to accomplish. A year of learning was lost, as well.

The firm's dilemma was compounded by a rolling, three-year strategic planning process. The most recent year's approved initiatives, obscured by their stealth cousins, and added to five previous years' active, stalled, backlogged, stealth, and inactive initiatives, produced serious confusion. What senior management thought was being worked on was completely different from what was actually being done.

When this dysfunction was discovered, the firm had a very difficult time discontinuing active, stalled, or shelved initiatives. There was a concern that terminating unit initiatives would anger SBU executives, who then might leave the firm. Corporate executives believed they could have it both ways—retain key executives *and* achieve the current year's financial targets in spite of the hodgepodge portfolio of initiatives. They expected to deal with the negative effects of the decision in the next planning cycle.

It took three or four years for the dysfunction to have an impact on the market value of the firm. By then the drop in value was quite obvious and resulted in greater scrutiny of the board of directors and senior management. New leadership was brought in for several of the business units, and a review of the strategic plans revealed the initiatives that should have been implemented. Corrective action was taken, and new initiatives, aided by a flurry of acquisitions, helped boost the performance shortfall. However, the initiative management problems intensified.

The attempted turnaround was accompanied with the rallying cry of a "return to basics." But the stock price continued to fall, and a new corporate CEO was announced. At this point, just about every initiative was scuttled and initiative development was begun anew. By now, the company had lost five to seven years of growth and learning.

While the downward spiral described in this case study was severe, the situation can get even worse. In fact, nearly every mid- to large-sized company experiences some of these problems. The only way out is to implement a sound initiative management process.

INITIATIVE MANAGEMENT: A BETTER WAY

A sound initiative management process sets the stage for firms to become fast, sleek wealth creators. The foundation of the process rests on two critical elements: (1) loading the initiative pipeline with active and backlogged initiatives and (2) categorizing each initiative in the portfolio.

Loading the Pipeline

Before loading the pipeline, initiatives are categorized as active or backlogged. The status of a given initiative is determined using the figure of merit (FOM) calculation, which was described briefly in Chapter 2. The formula for FOM is:

FOM = Expected Cash Benefit of the Initiative / Time to Complete / Cost to Complete

The simplest way to establish the numerator is to use expected revenue or cash flow. The estimated cash benefit is then divided by the estimated time and cost to complete the project. The resulting number can be used to rank order all the initiatives. Notice that this measure does not include prior investment in an initiative. Prior investment is important for other analyses, as in the original business case, but omitting it in the FOM calculation helps to block the tendency to keep initiatives in the portfolio too long. Thus, the FOM helps to eliminate pet initiatives that tend to stay around beyond their time and to terminate some unpromising initiatives, even if they have received large prior investment.

The formula shows that, to rank high in the FOM, an initiative must have a high benefit, with relatively low time and cost to complete. This automatically makes the initiative management process more action-oriented. While the formula is biased toward action, experience has shown that firms that depend on initiatives that require large investments and lengthy completion times (even though great benefits are expected) lose more often than they win.

Figure 4.1 contains a graphical representation of an initiative pipeline. The line that divides active and backlogged initiatives is determined by the amount of available resources in a given planning cycle. Simply add up the completion costs and draw a line when available resources are committed. Initiatives above the line are active and are to be put into play. Those below the line are considered to be in the backlog category and become active only when resources become available because an active initiative has been completed or terminated.

Figure 4.1
The Initiative Pipeline

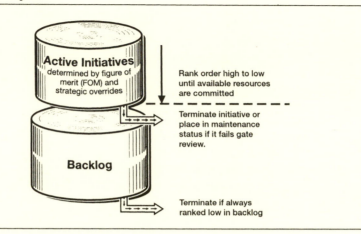

Source: Based on a methodology developed by the Thomas Group.

A strategic override feature protects initiatives that may not score as high in the FOM but that have prior customer commitment or are important to a more complex strategy. In this case, the executive oversight committee must agree that work on the initiative should continue.

One final point must be made regarding recently terminated initiatives. When an initiative is terminated before completion, the affected team will have learned significant lessons related to the reasons for the termination. In general, it is wise to maintain a repository of the business cases and other documentation related to all initiatives pursued in the seven most recent planning cycles.

If a significant cycle of learning is to evolve, a postmortem analysis of every initiative should include questions such as:

- Was the initiative terminated because of technological obsolescence?

- Was it terminated because a competitor entered the marketplace first or leapfrogged to an entirely new technology?

- Did internal culture barriers kill the initiative?

- Was there a shortage of people with the required new competencies?

Sometimes an initiative involves developing a technology that is ahead of its time. These initiatives can be put on hold and then quickly reinstated when market or customer forces change. Firms like Sharp keep new technology developments in a repository for up to 20 years.

Categorizing the Portfolio of Initiatives

The next step in the initiative management process is to categorize each initiative in the portfolio according to its *initial* vision, mission, strategy, and business case. "Too many cooks spoil the broth" is an old saying with much truth. When executive egos become involved in the journey of an initiative, its specifications can be inappropriately changed, costs can be run up, and the intended product can arrive very late to market. Having a simple, visible scheme for categorizing the initiatives helps everyone to stay focused on the original intent. Changing this intent then becomes a big decision. Sometimes it is better to terminate a conflicted initiative and start a new one with a new team rather than change the intent in mid-course. A sound initiative management process elevates these decisions to a central management committee and does not leave them open to a piecemeal approach.

Categorizing Individual Initiatives at One Point in Time

To depict the portfolio of initiatives at a given period in time, each one is coded as active or backlogged and then arrayed according to three dimensions:

1. Expected degree and complexity of growth and innovation. These initiatives help the company get better (improve incrementally), get bigger and broader (grow from current product and customer groups as "platforms" to launch new families of alternatives), or get bolder (make a breakthrough or change the rules of the competitive game).

2. Degree of new investment required and the relative degree of risk. Revenue growth initiatives may require little new investment and carry low risk; strategic initiatives may require moderate to high capital investment and carry the related risk; whole business generation initiatives could involve a large capital investment with high risk; and support initiatives may require low to moderate investment and carry low risk.

3. The initiative's expected direct impact (low, moderate, or high) on increasing shareholder wealth.

When all initiatives have been placed within the three-dimensional matrix, it is possible to evaluate how well they are balanced in strategic intent and impact (see Figure 4.2). It is important for both active and backlogged initiatives to be balanced within these dimensions at a given point in time. A concentration in one area of the 24 cells in the middle and upper levels of the matrix would be a sign of disproportionate strategic thrust. (We assume here that few initiatives would be considered if they promised to have only a low impact on shareholder wealth.)

Categorizing the Portfolio of Initiatives Through Time

The New Science of Strategy Execution recognizes that time is the only nonrecoverable resource. Companies can earn more money, build new facilities, or hire more people, but when a project consumes productive time, that time is gone forever. If an initiative does not produce new learning, some of the benefits that should have accrued will be lost and cannot be easily recovered. Successful

Figure 4.2
Categorizing Initiatives at One Point in Time

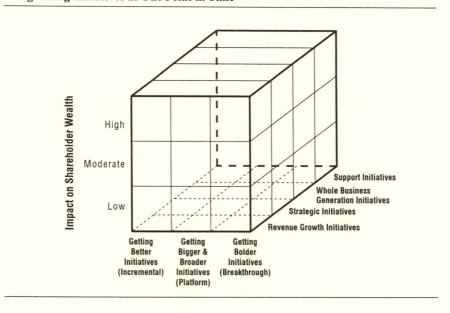

initiative management requires that initiatives be pursued within a context of continuous improvement in both profitable growth and innovation.

In today's labor market, knowledge workers want to work for companies that are focused on growth and innovation, and they will leave one firm for another to do so. Wall Street demands such a focus, as well. Even though a firm may briefly interrupt its growth and innovation journey in order to reengineer, reduce costs, or implement a turnaround, initiative management should continue to carry the mandate of growth and innovation. Healthy amounts of innovation and growth can improve the market value of the close followers of innovation as well as the pioneers.

The 4Bs of strategic intent (getting better, bigger, broader, or bolder) can be arrayed in a two-dimensional matrix that also requires continuous improvement. The graphic in Figure 4.3 contains practical examples of initiatives that may be customized for a firm's growth and innovation. The vertical axis indicates the degree of product innovation and the horizontal axis is related to the degree of customer innovation. The four cells within each quadrant are simply ways of teasing out more options.

Most firms array their portfolios of initiatives in the lower left portion of the diagram. But achieving long-term increases in market value requires that the firm travel a growth and innovation journey that eventually moves the portfolio from the lower left position to the upper right. Such movement in the portfolio will not take place overnight. Moving to the "getting bigger" and "getting broader" quadrants can lead to growth in market value while also providing essential learnings that will improve the chances of success in attempts at getting bolder.

Figure 4.3
Managing Continuous Profitable Growth and Innovation

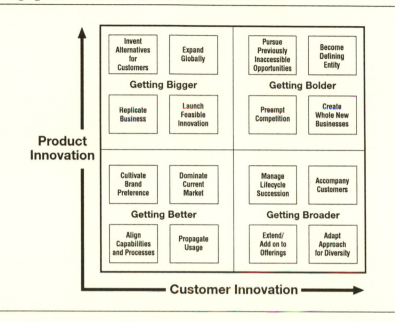

Source: Adapted from remarks made in 1995 by Les Alberthal, who was then chairman of EDS.

While the definition, pace, and path of the initiatives must be tailor-made for each company, the mandate remains. There must always be a balance of initiatives in the 16 cells of the matrix; however, the initiatives in the portfolio must lead cumulatively toward the upper right if market value is to be sustained.

THE INITIATIVE MANAGEMENT PROCESS

A variety of approaches have evolved over the past 20 years for managing new product development. Figure 4.4 shows the steps in the process as used in the New Science. The uniqueness of this model lies in the way organizational culture is used to push initiatives to completion as quickly as possible or to terminate them at the most prudent time. In order to progress from one phase to the next, an initiative must pass certain tests, such as the FOM test described earlier. Passing the test sends the initiative through the gate to the next phase; failure forces the initiative to be reworked or discarded.

Phase One: Scenario Generation

The first phase of the initiative management process is called scenario generation. The starting point for this phase is an initiative vision and strategy that are

Figure 4.4
Phases in the Initiative Management Process

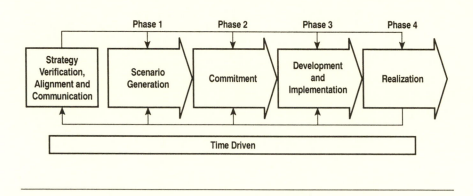

aligned, linked, and synchronized with the vision and strategy of the affected business unit. The end point of the phase is a detailed business case for the initiative and an evaluation using the figure of merit test. If the initiative satisfies these two criteria, it passes the first gate and moves into the second phase.

The way in which the first phase is implemented is critical to the success of the initiative management process. By doing background work to align the vision and strategy of the initiative with those of the business unit, the initiative team gives validity to the project and confirms that it presents a real opportunity. A very delicate balance must be maintained in this phase, because overly critical evaluation could inhibit future proposals with breakthrough potential. If rigid analysis and strong biases are applied too early in the process, only initiatives for incremental growth would be forthcoming, as they tend to be politically safe and easier to understand.

Figure 4.4 includes a time dimension that runs from left to right. Cycle times and calendar milestones of active initiatives must be intensely scrutinized from the start of a phase to its end. "First pass yield"—the percentage of initiatives proceeding through one phase to the next one with no rework—is also measured. In addition, all resource costs spent on the initiative during this time period are noted. Corrective action should be taken as early as possible when these measures are in violation of planned estimates.

Phase Two: Commitment

This phase begins with a brief, formal agreement between the initiative team and the central oversight committee that no "politics" will be involved in the further development of this initiative as it passes through the remaining phases. The choice of words can be company-specific, but if senior executives are serious about implementing world-class initiative management, they must purge the process of quarrelsome internal politics.

The end point of this phase is a rank-ordered, formally communicated, and prioritized commitment to develop and implement this initiative using the figure of merit process as a measurement. At this point, resources for the initiative have been formally approved and agreements about releasing initiative team members from prior accountabilities have been secured. It is key to note here that this phase, as we define it, is usually missing from most of the elaborate new product development processes alluded to at the beginning of this chapter. This phase is absolutely critical for the initiative management process to be successful and for world-class strategy execution to happen. If this phase is omitted, a key part of the foundation for the New Science of Strategy Execution will be missing.

Phase Three: Develop and Implement the Initiative

This phase begins with the formal announcement that the initiative has begun and the team is now accountable to the central executive committee. The end point of this phase is breakeven on all costs and investments and a final FOM test that allows the initiative to pass through the third gate to the last phase. The FOM for this gate is modified slightly to include measuring whether or not this initiative has gained enough competitive advantage to warrant continued funding through the fourth phase. It is possible for an initiative to break even, but not have generated enough advantage to see it through Phase Four. If this happens, the initiative could be terminated at once, or its content could be moved from the initiative management process into the routine work of the business unit.

Work in Phase Three draws on diplomacy, drive, and good project management. It also requires that the central management committee resolve any conflicts. In this phase, the initiative is launched for its intended customer groups (either external or internal) and the cycle time to reach breakeven is measured. Barriers must be removed and difficult work completed in order to push the initiative through this phase.

Phase Four: Realization

The beginning of this phase is really the end point of Phase Three—the successful launching of an initiative that has achieved breakeven on all resources expended, passed the phase gate FOM test, and achieved enough favorable competitive advantage to continue receiving funding. It has now been formally labeled a "Go Initiative," and it is expected to produce its planned financial return. For strategic and business generation initiatives, this achievement could mean fairly large, direct increases in the market value of the firm.

Receiving the label of a "Go Initiative" is a reward for successful teams. This phase can be the most arduous in the process, and the initiative team should be recognized for trying to navigate through the difficulties. Once an initiative begins to show an advantage in the marketplace, competitors will take notice and mount a counterattack. When this happens, the initiative team may have to reformulate certain aspects of the initiative if it is to achieve its planned financial return. Supply

chain costs may have to be lowered, repackaging may be needed for renewed differentiation, advertising may need to change, features may have to be enhanced,
and outbound logistics may have to improve the speed of response to customers.

Sometimes in this last phase, interest in the initiative begins to wane. If newer,
more exciting initiatives have been generated or released from backlog and are at the
beginning of their journey through the process, initiatives nearing completion may be
viewed as mundane. Being a Go Initiative can bring status and visibility to the project
and should encourage the team to drive on to achieve its ultimate financial goals.

MONITORING THE STATUS OF AN INITIATIVE

As an initiative passes through the phase/gate funnel, the team will need contributions from various executive, operating, and support processes and functions. For
example, a new product initiative may be categorized in the portfolio matrix as a
strategic initiative for getting broader with moderate impact on shareholder wealth.
It may currently reside in the "accompany customers" cell of the 4Bs chart. This initiative will probably require information and assistance from the customer relation-
ship/knowledge process in the generation phase, from a supply chain process in the
development/implementation phase, from a manufacturing/outbound logistics process in the realization phase, and from public relations in the realization phase. The
initiative may require championing from the strategy development process in generation and from the after-sales service and spare parts processes in realization. The
initiative team may ask for help from a strategic visioning process in the generation
phase and an ERP process in the development/implementation phase. It may need to
request that new competencies be identified and training developed from a people
development process in the development/implementation phase.

If the initiative management process is to work, it must also have an IT-enabled
capability to identify, measure, track, roll up, and forecast all-important quantita-
tive and qualitative metrics. The executive steering committee must be able to find
out what it needs to know about each initiative and the entire portfolio of initiatives
immediately upon request.

For individual initiatives, the following metrics must be available:

- Cycle times of individual contributing processes and total cycle times for all initiatives.

- Status of achievement against calendar milestones.

- First-pass yields (and the degree of rework initiatives experience by having to repeat a
  phase and a gate).

- All resource costs expended by the initiative.

The metrics can help to answer questions critical to good management, such as:

- Is the initiative on track to become what was intended in the business plan? If not, what
  should be done to change the vision, focus the effort, or terminate the project?

- What impact on shareholder wealth is currently expected?

- What barriers does the initiative face as it passes through the gates and phases?

- What is being learned during this initiative's journey?

- What new competencies have been developed that will help the initiative to produce winning results?

Additional measurements can help to answer questions related to tracking the portfolio of initiatives:

- Are the active initiatives in the phase/gate funnel well balanced among the phases? (Are there too many in the generation phase? In development/implementation?)

- What is the current mix of 4Bs—better, bigger, broader, bolder? Should the mix change?

- What is the current mix of growth, strategic, whole business generation, and support initiatives? Should the mix be changed?

- What is the cumulative total of expected contributions to increasing shareholder wealth? If a shortfall is detected, what action should be taken? Accelerate current initiatives? Terminate certain initiatives? Release selected initiatives from backlog? Formulate new initiatives?

CONTENTION MANAGEMENT AND EXECUTIVE ACTIVISM

Initiative management like true process management requires a central executive committee. Most companies or business units that have embraced true process management have a powerful central executive group made up of process owners with equal functional and geographic representation. There is no need to create another steering committee if such a committee already exists. The only modification that may be needed is to add specific mandates to the committee's charter. The following items should be added if they do not already exist.

1. *The mandate to appoint initiative owners and form initiative teams.* These teams are not permanent; they disband when the initiative achieves its planned financial performance in the realization phase or when the initiative is terminated. If the initiative is to succeed, these teams must be given the power to make decisions and act as required and the right to move across functional lines.

2. *The mandate to form cross-functional teams as barrier removal teams.* Members of these teams are trained in the art and science of identifying and removing subject matter, process, structure, and culture barriers that impede any progress in actualizing the initiative. This is a necessary but often revolutionary approach. In most firms, it would be a career-limiting move for any employee to identify, surface, and try to remove the barriers alone. This topic is covered more thoroughly in Chapter 9.

3. *The mandate to embrace contention management and executive activism as a way of life.* People must be allowed to disagree, as long as their concerns are mission-driven

and in line with shared objectives. Executive activism without acrimony is a key enabler to achieving world-class status as a fast, sleek wealth creator.

THE BENEFITS OF INITIATIVE MANAGEMENT

A sound initiative management process offers many benefits. These benefits include:

- Accelerating the positive financial impact of initiatives.

- Increasing margins due to higher price points or stabilizing prices in falling markets through speed of response with the right initiatives or being first to market.

- Increasing margins due to cost improvement by continuing to lower process cycle times, causing less rework, and synchronizing with market rhythms.

- Avoiding unnecessary expense in both working and fixed capital because work tends to be completed well the first time. Barriers are removed, stalls are highly visible, and there is simply no place to hide mistakes.

Sometimes, initiative owners have to leave a firm in order to launch a venture. But when the owner and team of a potentially successful initiative want to stay in-house, the initiative management process can help them proceed. Successful implementation of significant initiatives can be worth several times the current market value of the parent firm. For example, what would have been the value to Texas Instruments if it could have kept Compaq Computer or 12 Technologies in house? What would have been the value to IBM of holding onto Electronic Data Systems?

CONCLUSION

Initiative management is not just a fancy name. In practice, the process is more of a workhorse than a show horse. It can be the powerful catalyst for common sense strategic and operating management of a company that wants to become a fast, sleek wealth creator.

In the age of fast market rhythms, enabling technology, cross-functional teams, and capital looking for the highest expected return, sound initiative management integrates many previously separate aspects of strategic and operating control.

Chapter 5

Aligning Processes with Market Rhythms

In Chapter 3, we introduced the five key aspects of strategy execution: (1) initiative management, (2) aligning and synchronizing executive processes to market rhythms, (3) mapping the innovation journey, (4) understanding the constraints and opportunities in competition, and (5) managing the ripple effects and interdependencies of initiatives. In this chapter, we discuss the second of these aspects.

DEFINING EXECUTIVE PROCESSES

About 80 percent of the top management team's time and energy is spent on six critical executive processes and their linkages to the firm's operating and support processes. Some of these important processes nest a variety of subprocesses. Optimal strategy execution requires that these six key processes become "PALS" with operating and support processes and that all of them be linked and synchronized with the firm's market rhythm. As shown in the chart in Figure 5.1, the high priority processes are (1) strategic management/governance, (2) strategy alignment, (3) growth/strategic initiatives, (4) opportunity cycle management, (5) organization structure change, and (6) pre- and post-M&A integration. These processes are intended to provide the strategic direction for and commitment to all operating and support processes.

In most established firms, however, there is huge opportunity to drastically improve these executive processes. Such an improvement would also make a large contribution to effecting world-class strategy execution. In the prevailing view, executive processes are expected to provide vision, direction, governance, control, and risk management; and we agree that these deliverables are still required. Nevertheless, our audits and work with clients indicate that it is in the area of true commitment to the operating and support processes that executives can make their main contribution to world-class strategy execution. If these executive processes remain aloof from and cause interference with the operating and support processes, they create a major barrier to execution success.

Figure 5.1
Executive, Operating, and Support Processes

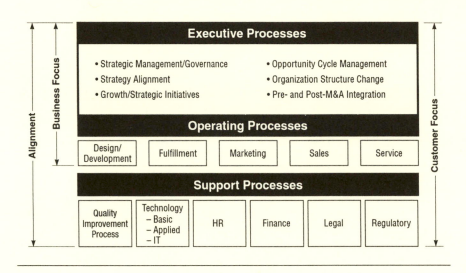

Analysis and improvement of executive processes has been lacking in many established firms for a number of reasons.

1. The executive office or corporate center has never been challenged to create true recurring processes.

2. The work of the executive office is usually taken for granted as satisfactory, but the new mandate to provide true year-to-year commitment to the operating and support processes demands that executive processes be improved to contribute added value to the firm.

3. Until now, there has been no set of tools to help improve executive processes.

4. As we will show, the improvement potential is large and quantifiable.

In devising the tools for executive process improvement, we have coined the acronym PALS. The acronym describes the four essential relationships among these processes. That is, they must be prioritized, aligned, linked, and synchronized with operating and support processes and with the firm's market rhythm. For clarity, we define these basic imperatives as follows:

• *Prioritized:* rated in order of preference or importance; indicating superior standing or position.

• *Aligned:* positioned in the correct relative position.

• *Linked:* connected or joined, as the links of a chain.

• *Synchronized:* timed to be compatible, supportive, and consistent.

Strategic Management/Governance

The strategic management and governance process is one of the primary executive processes. It occurs in three phases, each of which contains a number of subprocesses as shown in Figure 5.2.

The Strategic Phase

The first phase in this executive process establishes the organization's corporate strategy and the shape of each business unit's strategy, that is, the major focus of the strategy, such as speed of delivery, services provided, cost of production, product quality, or innovative solutions. This phase includes a number of steps or subprocesses: (1) assessing external forces that are affecting the business; (2) gathering up-to-date knowledge about customers and understanding the company's relationship with its customers; (3) clarifying the corporate vision and the strategic filter that guide the identification and selection of new opportunities and initiatives; (4) establishing the organization's strategic direction and strategic intent; and (5) developing strategies and a planning process for sectors, groups, and SBUs. In this phase, decisions are made about the value of forming relationships to create an extended community of suppliers, vendors, and customers.

The strategic phase is also the time when executives must determine the role and management style of the corporate center and decide how conflicts among business units, departments, and processes will be handled. Conflict resolution, contention management, and executive activism are key leadership skills that must be applied here if the firm is to work toward world-class strategy execution.

The Planning Phase

The second phase in strategic management and governance involves creating plans for functional and geographic areas, planning for technology, and allocating resources. When these plans are approved, the next phase begins.

The Implementation Phase

The final phase in this executive process consists of three extensive subprocesses: (1) initiative management and continuous process improvement, (2) the on-going process of measuring and managing performance, and (3) validating, modifying, and closing gaps in financial and operating performance. (Notice here the importance of initiative management as discussed in Chapter 4.)

Figure 5.2 depicts the three phases as a recurring process flow chart while overlaying the timing of involvement with key functional areas, as an example of the many ways these steps might be customized according to a given company's needs.

Defining executive responsibilities as processes makes it possible to monitor them according to standard process measures—cycle time, amount of rework, and cost. The steps shown in the flow chart can be used as a "strawman" against which any firm's executive processes can be mapped for sequencing and interrelationships.

Figure 5.2
The Strategic Management/Governance Process

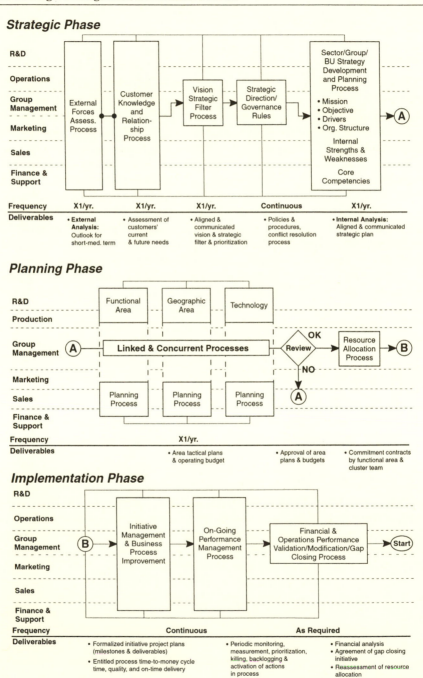

These processes contain great potential for improvement, and most firms have not even begun to scrutinize them as they have their operating and support processes.

Thinking of strategic responsibilities as processes also helps to relate them to the firm's market rhythm. Subprocesses that do not meet the PALS requirements regarding market rhythms become obvious and can be corrected immediately. Synchronizing these subprocesses with the rhythms of the marketplace puts the firm's strategic management and governance into a dynamic flow. If the processes are enabled by technology, they can respond automatically to the rhythm of the market, eliminating the spikes of activity experienced in a linear, calendar-based mode.

Linking the strategic processes with the firm's operating and support processes helps to create a systemic architecture that can inform and support all the decisions and actions that guide the firm toward its intended future. When implemented correctly, this systemic architecture can be a source of advantage over competitors who cling to the outmoded view that the executive work of the firm cannot be improved. Figure 5.3 describes the complex relationship among these processes when matched against the phases in initiative management.

The executive, operating, and support processes of every firm must be defined in a manner that allows their cross impacts to be measured and understood. Tables 5.1.a and 5.1.b list 30 key executive, operating, and support processes as they were defined for one client. This list can be used to analyze and evaluate a firm's current processes. Tables 5.2.a and 5.2.b show how these processes can be assessed in terms of formal mapping, frequency, restrictive barriers, and perhaps the most complex but also the most important, key cross impacts. The power of the New Science is achieved only when executive processes are assessed for their guidance and commitment to the operating and support processes. Identifying existing cross impact and barriers is critical to understanding how the suite of executive processes helps or hinders the PALS relationship with market rhythm, with other processes, and within the suite itself. This analysis is the essential starting place for eliminating or combining processes to create a fast, sleek wealth creating firm.

Using this approach to process analysis allows a firm to enhance its world-class execution status by doing away with one or more of the subprocesses related to strategic management/governance. For example, the time spent on budgeting and producing an annual operating plan can be eliminated by moving to a rolling, 13-month sales forecast that is tied to a fluid chart of accounts. In this way, budgeting and resource allocation shift from an inflexible, once-a-year nightmare to a dynamic process that adjusts according to the dictates of the market rhythm. Even if processes are not eliminated, they must be simplified and refined to support the highly time-sensitive strategic management/governance process.

Strategy Alignment

The second executive process seeks to ensure that all parts of the firm's strategic efforts are aligned and in tune with the rhythmic flow of the business. It offers an organized way to avoid the inevitable actions and events that tend to work against alignment.

Figure 5.3
Aligning, Linking, and Synchronizing Processes with Initiative Management

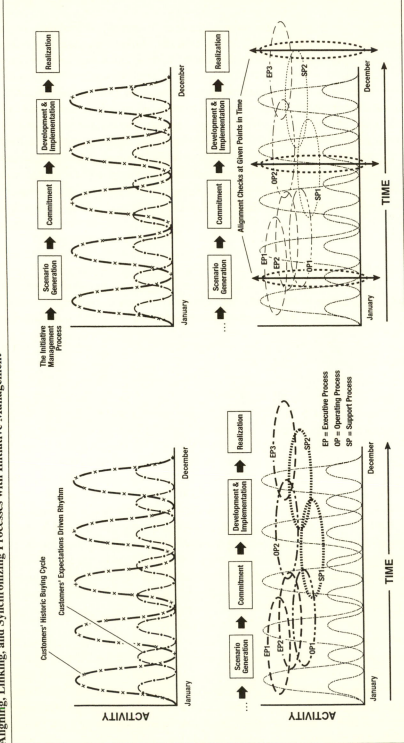

Table 5.1.a
Defining Executive Processes

Executive Processes

Strategic Phase	Planning Phase	Implementation Phase
External Forces Assessment Process Assesses threats and opportunities in the external environment.	Functional Area Planning Process Drives the direction from the processes in the Strategic Phase into the functional areas.	Initiative Management Process Generates, commits to, implements to breakeven, and realizes to ultimate planned return key strategic initiatives consistent with direction set in previous processes.
Customer Knowledge and Relationships Process Develops relationships between key customers and executives and tries to establish *your firm* as the vendor of choice. This process also seeks to identify and understand latent, emerging customer needs before competitors can.	Geographic Area Planning Process Drives the direction from the processes in the Strategic Phase into the geographic areas. Technology Planning Process Plans leader or follower technology of all kinds consistent with established strategic direction.	Performance Management Process Assesses planned versus actual numbers, puts the right people in the right jobs, and establishes the charter for a steering committee to oversee the timely execution of all initiatives and plans.
Vision and Strategic Filter Process Establishes the field of vision for the next three planning cycles and puts in place a strategic filter that rules certain opportunities in or out.	Overarching Operating Processes Planning Process Seeks to integrate and synchronize all operating processes with all executive processes to ensure processes true commitment in resource allocation over time.	Financial Performance Gap-Closing Process Targets key income and balance sheet accounts to close any gaps between planned and actual performance. The process also takes corrective measures within the governance rules established earlier.
Strategic Direction/Governance Rules Process Systematically assesses strengths, weaknesses, threats and opportunities over a rolling three-year window and begins to narrow the direction for the first year of the plan. This process also sets out governance rules that seek agreement about authority and dispute resolution.	Revenue Forecasting and Business Case Development Process Validates accurate revenue forecasts and develops a business case for achieving set revenue goals. Annual Operating Planning Process Integrates and synchronizes all yearly revenue, expense, and capital expenditure commitments.	Multidirectional and Inter-unit Communications Process Ensures communication with anyone at anytime and anywhere about all of the above decisions and actions.
Sector/Business Unit Strategy Development Process Takes direction from the first four executive processes and focuses planning on levels further down in the organization.	Resource Allocation Process Includes budgeting process, approves revenue and profit commitments, and allocates working and fixed capital expenditures.	

49

Table 5.1.b
Defining Operating and Support Processes

Operating Processes	Support Processes
Customer Relationship Management Process Seeks to keep active, on-line, real-time communication with customers concerning current needs and the products and services *your firm* offers. Database warehouses with expert trending systems are usually part of this process.	**Human Resources Process** Selects, develops, rewards, and retains people with the right core competencies, values, and other desired attributes. The goal is to build the value of people.
New Product/Service Development Process Seeks to design and develop products and services to a *known* customer need, ensuring desired quality and required price points.	**Information Technology Process** Ensures the appropriate hardware and software required for the cost effective and timely storage, dissemination, retrieval, and use of information that gives the required depth, breadth, and richness of information required to widen the firm's competitive advantage.
Supply Chain Process Seeks maximum PALS (prioritized, aligned, linked, and synchronized) status with the speed and demands of the market and among procurement, in-bound logistics, WIP inventory, production, warehousing, distribution. logistics, and real-time location/status assessment and reporting so that cycle time, rework, cost, and customer satisfaction are optimized.	**Quality Process** Ensures that customers continue to receive the product and service value and satisfaction they have come to expect.
Total Supply Chain Management Process Seeks to seamlessly link favored suppliers, vendors, alliances, joint ventures, and customers for total network accessibility, leverage, and competitive advantage.	**Legal Process** Supports the risk management of the firm.
Marketing Process Attempts to gain visibility, induce trial, build brand equity and provide information on the value proposition (features, benefits, and price) *your firm* offers. The process also helps to find qualified buyers.	**Regulatory Process** Attempts within the norms of law and ethics to understand and react to the dynamic flow of regulation that affects the industry and the firm.
Sales Process Builds a pipeline of qualified sales opportunities, prioritizes them, and measures cycle time, rework, hit rate, and revenue and margin data.	**Lobbying Process** Attempts within the norms of law and ethics to influence the dynamic flow of regulation that affects the industry and the firm.
Customer Financing/Credit Process Extends funds to customers and is part of the total value proposition offered.	
Customer Service Process Serves as the front line in handling the entire customer experience pre-sale, during sale, and after-sale service. The process includes billing and collections.	

50

Table 5.2.a
Assessing Executive Process Interaction

Which of the following executive processes does your firm use formally? Indicate your answer with a ✔.	Not Used	Used	Time Interval			What kinds of barriers affect this process?				What other processes interact the most with this process?
			1XYr.	4XYr.	Continuous	Subject Matter	Process	Structure	Culture	
Strategic Phase										
External Forces Assessment										
Customer Knowledge and Relationships										
Vision and Strategic Filter										
Strategic Direction/Governance Rules										
Sector/Business Unit Strategy Development										
Planning Phase										
Functional Area Planning										
Geographic Area Planning										
Technology Planning										
Overarching Operating Processes Planning										
Revenue Forecasting and Business Case Development										
Annual Operating Planning										
Resource Allocation										
Implementation Phase										
Initiative Management										
Performance Management										
Financial Performance Gap-Closing										
Multidirectional and Inter-Unit Communication										
Other Processes										

Table 5.2.b
Assessing Operating and Support Process Interaction

Which of the following operating and support processes does your firm use formally? Indicate your answer with a ✔.	Not Used	Used	Time Interval			What kinds of barriers affect this process?				What other processes interact the most with this process?
			1XYr.	4XYr.	Continuous	Subject Matter	Process	Structure	Culture	
Operating Processes										
Customer Relationship Management										
New Product/Service Development										
Supply Chain										
Procurement										
In-bound Logistics										
WIP Inventory										
Production										
Warehousing										
Distribution										
Logistics										
Real-time Location/Status										
Total Supply Chain Management										
Marketing										
Customer Financing/Credit										
Customer Service										
Support Processes										
Human Resources										
Information Technology										
Quality										
Legal										
Regulatory										
Lobbying										
Other Processes										

Figure 5.4 shows the eight elements that must be carefully aligned to ensure that allocated resources (dollars, people, technology, etc.) are being used to produce the intended strategic results. The strategic elements can be tested for alignment by answering a few key questions and assessing the consistency of the answers. Begin by examining the alignment between the first two elements: Purpose and Vision. Then review their alignment with Mission. When these three are aligned, move on to Business Drivers. Proceed through the elements, comparing one new element at a time, until complete alignment has been achieved.

Purpose

Is the firm a saleable asset, or is it an asset to be passed on to future generations of managers? This definition of purpose is the rock-bottom foundation for strategic alignment. If this factor is not completely consistent with the other factors, there is almost no chance for real strategy alignment. There will always come a time to sell a business, but if senior management is not honest on this point, all the elements of the strategic process will not be aligned. There have been instances in which companies have instituted all-inclusive procedures for preparing elaborate vision and mission statements defining the firm as a legacy to be passed on to future generations of family or leadership. While at the same time, a small group of powerful executives was trying to sell the business. When a business's purpose changes from legacy to saleable asset, many of the elements that follow would have to be changed as well. Of course, selling a business cannot be openly discussed during the deal process, so the challenge is to find a way to begin aligning the other elements as soon as possible, and to communicate accordingly.

Vision

Over the next three to five years, what is the firm's intent regarding customers, shareholders, competitors, suppliers, employees, and interest groups? What criteria does the firm use to identify and select new strategic opportunities and initiatives?

Mission

What clear, succinct statement describes what will be accomplished by the united efforts of people, assets, technology, and processes over the planning period?

Business Drivers

How does the underlying economic model of the business dictate revenue, cost, profit, and capital and risk requirements? The way a company defines its approach to scale, scope, and time is determined by the market size required to compete successfully in an industry. Scale refers to how big the company needs to be. Scope describes how far a dollar of marketing expense can be spread over diverse products or brands. Time drivers flow in part from the scale and scope drivers and describe how time (in addition to market rhythm) must be viewed, for example, seasonally, monthly, or daily, in order to serve customers' real requirements.

Figure 5.4
Strategic Alignment Elements

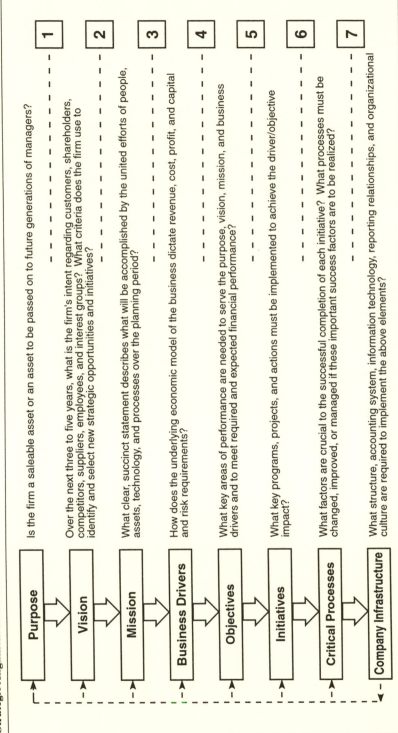

Purpose	Is the firm a saleable asset or an asset to be passed on to future generations of managers?	1
Vision	Over the next three to five years, what is the firm's intent regarding customers, shareholders, competitors, suppliers, employees, and interest groups? What criteria does the firm use to identify and select new strategic opportunities and initiatives?	2
Mission	What clear, succinct statement describes what will be accomplished by the united efforts of people, assets, technology, and processes over the planning period?	3
Business Drivers	How does the underlying economic model of the business dictate revenue, cost, profit, and capital and risk requirements?	4
Objectives	What key areas of performance are needed to serve the purpose, vision, mission, and business drivers and to meet required and expected financial performance?	5
Initiatives	What key programs, projects, and actions must be implemented to achieve the driver/objective impact?	6
Critical Processes	What factors are crucial to the successful completion of each initiative? What processes must be changed, improved, or managed if these important success factors are to be realized?	7
Company Infrastructure	What structure, accounting system, information technology, reporting relationships, and organizational culture are required to implement the above elements?	

Objectives

What key areas of performance are needed to serve the purpose, vision, mission, and business drivers and to meet required and expected financial performance? Quantifiable objectives should be the mirror image of the real business drivers.

Initiatives

What key programs, projects, and actions must be implemented to achieve the driver/objective impact?

Critical Processes

What factors are crucial to the successful completion of each initiative? What processes must be changed, improved, or managed if these important success factors are to be realized? How do these processes interrelate and cross impact to help drive initiatives through the initiative management process?

Company Infrastructure

What structure, accounting system, information technology, reporting relationships and organizational culture are required to implement the above elements?

Most firms experience some degree of misalignment in these critical elements. This problem may be caused by entrepreneurial efforts within the subdivisions of an organization. More often, however, it is caused by a lack of accountability and clutter in a dysfunctional strategic management/governance process. Dysfunction allows "stealth initiatives" to be funded and pursued, even though they may not fit into the purpose, vision, or mission of the company. These initiatives soak up resources, time, and employee effort that could be better spent on more aligned initiatives. Alignment, therefore, is crucial for leveraging resources for achieving optimal financial results.

The fourth panel of Figure 5.3 notes the requirement of periodic alignment checks of the above elements in the midst of what appears to be absolute chaos caused by the interaction of market rhythm, dynamic process cycles, and the pursuit of initiatives through the initiative management process. This appearance of chaos helps to demonstrate visually why strategy execution is so difficult and why mastering it can be a huge source of value creation for firms. Figures 5.3 and 5.4 depict the very essence of the New Science.

Revenue Growth/Strategic Initiatives

The third major executive process tracks the company's revenue growth and strategic initiatives. This process ensures that initiatives are being generated, committed to, implemented to breakeven, and realized to the required level of return at the speed and quantity necessary to grow the market value of the firm. This process was discussed completely in the previous chapter. It is mentioned here to distinguish between revenue growth initiatives and strategic initiatives and to show how these two types of initiatives relate to the other executive processes.

Revenue growth initiatives allow the firm to focus exclusively on quick, profitable revenue growth. These initiatives *do not* require new net investment, although investment is almost always reallocated among key operating processes. In working with clients, we have found that profitable, top-line growth often stalls because there is an imbalance in investment and resources among the processes of new product development, sales and marketing, and fulfillment. The key factor here is the reallocation of resources—without new net investment—to the priorities that customers care about.

Strategic initiatives focus on profitable growth, but they also focus on the other drivers of shareholder wealth—operational costs, capital investment, risk, the tax rate, and the cost of capital. These initiatives *always* require new net investment.

For many firms, revenue growth initiatives are the "low hanging fruit." These projects move through the initiative management process quickly and easily. Strategic initiatives, on the other hand, are often more difficult and test the process because of interference by internal, political concerns. Experience has shown that these concerns lessen as confidence in the process grows.

In most companies, approved operational initiatives are managed within the walls of specific organizational units, even though recent theory related to supply chain management suggests that a cross-boundary approach often works better. The initiative management process, on the other hand, bridges the organizational structure and helps to manage cross-unit, cross-functional, or cross-territory resources so that initiatives are developed and implemented at the world-class tempo set by new entrants. New entrants have the luxury of asking the classic strategy question: "If we were not already in business, what business would we enter today?" The initiative management processes we present in this book can help a firm break through its dysfunction and strategize as freely as those new entrants.

Opportunity Cycle Management

This executive process is another type of initiative management, and it builds from the methods of developing revenue growth and strategic initiatives described here. Opportunity cycle management is often found in firms that stay competitive by reinventing themselves every five to seven years or in those that are so skilled in strategy execution that they can repeatedly create whole new businesses for changing the rules of the competitive game. These firms are operating in the *Getting Bolder* quadrant of the 4Bs chart. This approach is of special use for firms that are coming under severe fire from three tough market realities: (1) ever-shortening opportunity cycles in the marketplace, making speed paramount; (2) customer demand for more complex linkages of product, service, and technology infrastructure; (3) the threat of major new competitors.

To operationalize opportunity cycle management, executives must view their firm as a "portfolio of real business opportunities." In many cases, the process is used to produce a steady stream of potential opportunities that can then be assessed against established strategic and alignment criteria. In other instances, the corporate center chooses to seed diverse opportunities as a way of gaining real options for the future. While it is typical to minimize capital expenditure by developing these diverse options as alliances or joint ventures, firms such as Virgin Atlantic have set a fast pace in making repeated capital commitments for new businesses. We will probably see more of this strategy in the future, especially in industries like retail where multiple store formats can be launched. Troubled Kmart, for example, might choose to extend its investment in the Martha Stewart brand by creating a Martha Stewart Boutique as a stand-alone opportunity. Whatever the strategic intent, all potential opportunities must pass through the initiative management process, just as other initiatives do.

The final step in the opportunity management process is to sum the revenue contributions of all candidates and initiatives in the pipeline. If there is a shortfall in total yield, steps must be taken to close the gaps. The executive team may decide to:

- Speed up the processing of current opportunities,

- Activate selected opportunities in backlog, or

- Find or create new candidates.

In choosing among the possibilities in the three types of strategic action—revenue growth initiatives, strategic initiatives, and opportunity cycle management, a CEO must carefully assess a company's external challenges and internal capabilities and then decide just how much change should be unleashed on the organization. Actions for revenue growth are probably the least disruptive, while opportunity cycle management is the most challenging.

Opportunity cycle management requires everyone in the organization, regardless of unit affiliation, to maintain an entrepreneurial mindset and to play a cross-unit, time-synchronized role in making sure selected opportunity candidates increase the market value of the firm. In effect, this process comes close to creating a form of corporate governance similar to a venture-holding company.

Changing Organizational Structure

Organizational structure is a useless word in a process-dominated company. In a world of perfectly designed processes that are linked and synchronized with the rhythms of the marketplace, structure would be unnecessary.

As yet, however, we know of no purely process organizations; thus, structure still plays a role. The major bases of structure—product, customer, technology, geography, and project—serve to focus people and resources on doing a specific job. Structure left unchanged for too long, however, manifests bureaucracy, inertia, and dogma.

In practicing the New Science of Strategy Execution, structure must be defined as the way in which people, resources, and technology are combined so that their work will have the greatest impact at the most critical times—and those times must be determined by a firm's marketplace rhythm. Structure defines discrete quantities of work within the system of executive processes. The goal is to deliver repeated, winning thrusts of work. Because so many executive processes are customer- and competitor-facing, the New Science view of structure folds the "new" into important routine work efforts.

Optimal procedures for changing organizational structure should be based on the first four executive processes—strategic management and governance, strategy alignment, revenue growth and strategic initiatives, and opportunity cycle management. If these processes are functioning properly, the timing and nature of structural change will be readily apparent.

It is absolutely vital to the implementation of the New Science that the structure of the organization be based on the crucial initiative work rather than on the day-to-day work of the company. This shift is supported by today's technology capabilities:

- The rise of company intranets and group software.

- The creation of interactive database, storage and retrieval capabilities.

- The automation of performance reviews and evaluations that are employee-initiated and include input from peers and superiors in appropriate communities of interest.

Current technologies allow work groups for routine operations to change quickly and seamlessly. Employees can move from job to job, while their personal and job-related records remain intact. The only caveat is that there continue to be a way to measure returns on productive assets, such as plants, distribution centers, and warehouses, and that a portion of those returns follow personnel who may be assigned to one cost code today and another tomorrow.

Structuring a firm's organization to its initiative work is a key principle of the New Science. Grouping clusters of tasks into high performance teams moves the portfolio of initiatives through the management process at world-class speed and ensures that planned financial returns will be achieved as quickly as possible. Such a dynamic view of structure turns the static noun form of the word into a verb—structuring. Jack Welch, the former CEO of GE, is quoted as saying that, over time, a business should "structure to meet the interfaces with the market." The New Science process of organizational structure, when placed within the context of the other executive processes, provides a new way of solving the structuring dilemma.

Pre- and Post-M&A Integration

Like the dilemma of organizational structure, integration issues arising before and after a merger or acquisition have been around for a long time. These issues are addressed as a major executive process because making a successful acquisition can be almost a full-time job. Sometimes executives in a top management team become so caught up in the "thrill of the hunt" they virtually ignore their responsibilities in the other processes. It is as though they become addicted to identifying targets, courting and pricing them, and negotiating and closing deals.

There is no doubt that the acquisitions process is exciting. However, the value of executive work is in balancing all six of the major executive processes, not focusing on one. In a client company, we observed how the all-out pursuit of just one major acquisition brought about huge unintended changes in other processes. The teams from the acquiring and target companies deluged each other with so many requirements that every executive process was incrementally changed. This, in turn, changed the acquiring company's process alignment, linkage, mutual reinforcement, and fit with the customer-driven rhythm of the marketplace. The company's productivity was in gridlock for almost 14 months.

Because the potential ripple effects of pre- and post-M&A integration, the New Science requires that the screening criteria for new targets include an analysis of the target's fit with the acquiring company's major executive processes.

ALIGNING AND LINKING EXECUTIVE, OPERATING, AND SUPPORT PROCESSES

The entire process architecture of a company is shown again in Figure 5.5. The executive processes are listed vertically, and the operating and support processes are shown across the base. The gears in the graphic design imply that all executive process must be linked and aligned in order to provide the necessary leadership for the other processes. The gear metaphor extends to include all operating and support processes because the challenges of the present business environment make these processes strategic as well. A process change anywhere in the system can cause ripple effects in the work processes of one or more of the other units in the organization.

Figure 5.5
The Process Architecture of a Company

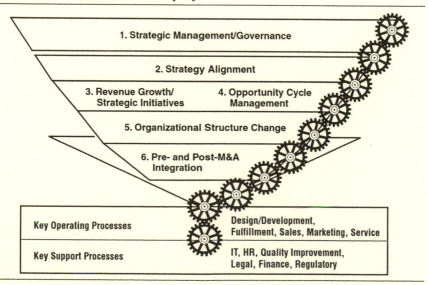

In Chapter 2, we told the story of a company that makes medical imaging products, but its last four products were denied FDA approval. This company is a good example of how a lack of interconnectedness in processes can have injurious effects. When we audited the firm's strategic management/governance process, we found such confusion and short-circuiting of the various subprocesses that the cycle time in new product development totaled seven to ten years. With lobbying, the cycle time could eventually get to three years—but this would be well into the future. Company executives were brooding over this issue, rather than focusing on the fact that the customer-driven rhythm was three months based on a buying cycle of once a year. They should have put their attention on initiatives that were PALS with the market rhythm reality, instead of spending time on the problems with new product development. Figure 5.6 summarizes the findings of the complete audit and compares them to the capabilities of a more flexible new entrant.

Figure 5.6
Baseline Diagnosis vs. New Entrant Capabilities

Baseline Findings	*Required Future State*
• The strategic management/ governance (SM/G) processes are *not mutually reinforcing.*	*Skills of Major New Entrants* • Speed
	• Success rate
• The SM/G processes are *not in sync with the timing and rhythms* of the marketplace.	• Commitment
	• Desire
• The SM/G processes *cause confusion, delay, and frustration* in the operating processes. **◄GAP►**	• Clarity
	• Simplicity
	• Linkage/Alignment
• The SM/G processes *give little direction and priority* for the support processes.	• Tenacity
	• Communication
• Too much is going on; *initiative overload* with little courage to kill outdated or ineffective initiatives.	• Continuous learning
• Too much bureaucracy *causes delays in making true resource commitments.*	
• *Little sense of urgency,* "This too shall pass."	
• Too much analysis with *too few results.*	
• *Processes are performed in "ivory tower" isolation* with little market-based reality.	

BECOMING PALS WITH MARKET RHYTHMS

A number of steps must be taken if processes are to continue to be PALS, that is, prioritized, aligned, linked, and synchronized with each other and with market rhythms over time. Executives can use the following checklist to revise and maintain these critical relationships:

1. Remove all executive, operating, and support processes that cause the firm to be out of synchronization with the market rhythm. The work of these processes should be eliminated or combined in a leaner form with other processes.

2. Shorten the cycle times and increase the yields of all remaining relevant executive, operating, and support processes. Customize IT to automate these processes.

3. Practice world-class initiative management as outlined in Chapter 4.

4. Allow the owners of an initiative or opportunity to request resources from the various process owners as needed during the four phases of the initiative process.

5. Remember that for a firm to hedge its bets in today's business environment, the various types of initiatives and opportunities must complete the four-stage initiative management process at a rate of four to five times the pace of the market rhythm. Time to completion must be measured and tracked as a key operational metric.

6. Provide at market rhythm tempo or upon demand to the initiative team and the central oversight committee all appropriate information on contributing executive, operating, and functional/support processes. This information gives the firm's leaders an important bird's-eye view of progress and helps them to manage risk accurately.

CONCLUSION

The factors discussed in this chapter are the building blocks business leaders can use to help their firms become fast, sleek wealth creators. At this point in the unfolding of the New Science of Strategy Execution, a firm could, enabled with the proper information technology, be about 60 percent of the way to world-class strategy execution status. That is, if the company were to practice great project management, use the initiative management process with world-class skill, and make all executive, operating, and support processes true PALS with market rhythms, almost two-thirds of the journey to world-class execution status would be accomplished.

The next chapter adds to these skills by presenting a way to think about, map, and execute a path to growth and continuous improvement.

Chapter 6

The Journey to Growth and Continuous Improvement

The concept of growth and continuous improvement is crucial to the New Science of Strategy Execution. Because time is the only nonrecoverable resource, it is a professional imperative for business leaders to pursue initiative management with a requirement for continuous growth, innovation, and improvement. Even though a firm may pause momentarily on its growth and innovation journey to perform reengineering, cost reduction, or turnaround type thrusts (the subject of the next chapter), the mandate for growth and innovation should always be present.

In Chapter 4, we introduced the 4Bs diagram (shown again as Figure 6.1). The matrix shows 16 possible options a firm may choose in growing better, bigger, broader, or bolder. Experience has shown that most firms array their portfolio of initiatives somewhere in the lower left portion of the matrix (getting better). However, increasing the market value of the firm requires maintaining a balance of initiatives in all the diagram's cells, while following a growth and innovation journey that moves from the lower left segment to the upper right. In fact, *the seven stages of growth and continuous improvement that we describe here are a key delivery vehicle for traversing the 4Bs for growth, innovation, and strategic advantage.*

This chapter presents a roadmap of the seven stages of growth and continuous improvement that have been gleaned from years of consulting, testing, and research. Its genesis was during a four-year stint as head of strategy development for five client firms that included observations of key strategic changes and their impacts. The framework is offered as a model for executives to use as a comparison in assessing a firm's path to growth and improvement, and to assist them in recognizing the pitfalls and barriers that may be encountered along the way. While all firms will differ to some degree in how they traverse this journey, the seven stages provide an excellent starting point from which to assess the effectiveness of a current process and, if necessary, to design a more useful path for the future.

Before reading this chapter, it may be helpful to consider the following questions:

• What does your firm's path to growth and continuous improvement look like?

Figure 6.1
The 4 Bs of Innovation and Growth

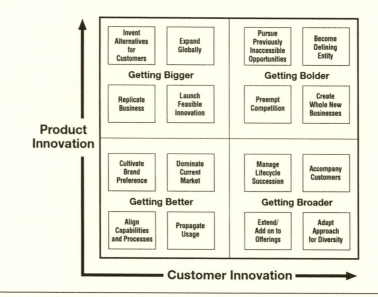

Source: Adapted from remarks made in 1995 by Les Alberthal, who was then chairman of EDS.

- How have the stages in that process changed throughout your firm's history?

- What will your journey look like as you move into the future?

- What barriers may emerge along the way?

- How would you go about identifying and removing barriers at world-class speed?

- What role do you believe leaders and managers must play in improving the future journey?

THE SEVEN STAGES OF GROWTH AND CONTINUOUS IMPROVEMENT

The road to growth and continuous improvement has seven discrete stages and several identifiable transition phases that must occur between the stages. When viewed as a single entity, the seven stages comprise a never-ending cycle (see Figure 6.2). Some firms complete each stage successfully and use their excess cash flow to launch whole new businesses beginning again at Stage 1. Other firms do not traverse the stages well—they either become stuck on their journey and retreat before moving forward again, or disappear because they fail completely or are acquired by a stronger firm.

Figure 6.2
The Seven Stages of Growth and Continuous Improvement

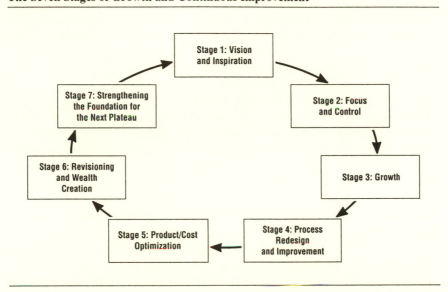

The duration of the stages and the transitional periods cannot be stated precisely. It depends on the timing of the average market rhythm in the industry. The market rhythm may be days, as in some retail settings, or it may extend to 12 or 18 months, as in business-to-business transactions and the industrial equipment industry. The New Science requires that a firm's movement through the stages be calibrated to its particular market rhythm. As the firm completes each cycle of learning throughout the seven stages, the pace must be increased to match the standard speed of new entrants. New entrants will always set a very fast pace because they have not yet developed significant process and culture barriers. Sometimes, as in the case of events such as the tragedy of September 11, 2001, market rhythms and the speed of traversing the seven stages slows down for everyone. Thus, dynamic timing and sensitivity is a focal point in the New Science of Strategy Execution.

Stage 1: Vision and Inspiration

The journey begins with the founding of the company or new business unit—the moment when the principals in a venture have found a niche of demand for their product or service and enough funding for the start-up. Stage 1 is characterized by a sense of excitement, enthusiasm, and exuberance. The principals have attracted like-minded people to the venture and the group's chemistry is uplifting. If the real odds of success were known, probably no one would proceed beyond this point, but the principals in the venture think their idea is a guaranteed "sure thing." As a result, they move through barriers with energy and optimism, believing that it is only time until they succeed.

Something magical happens at this stage. There is novelty, an upbeat environment, and just the right amount of hard work. Customers become excited, too, and it seems that nothing is impossible. The firm moves into an explosive ramp-up, while still burning cash—hopefully at planned levels. It is here that the leaders of the firm sometimes begin to assess a variety of opportunities that extend the original business idea. These extensions seem to pop up unbidden because of the "buzz" around the firm and its impending success.

Transition to Focus and Control

Eventually, the amount of work that had been taken on so willingly begins to swamp the capacity of the available people, processes, and technology. Cash flow may still be negative and the next round of financing may be too expensive in terms of equity dilution or interest rate. For the first time, fear and concern surface, accompanied by sadness and regret that the wonderful exuberant stage of vision and inspiration has to end.

Stage 2: Focus and Control

In the second stage, the new firm tries to "have its cake and eat it, too." Success breeds rivals, and a number of potential competitors may enter the market. The firm's leaders begin to think hard about a total strategy that might ensure a sustainable competitive advantage. They may have to retreat a bit or give up a planned advance and settle into a position that can be protected for a while. The next round of financing is usually gained through a combination of means—additional equity (the least preferred route) and affordable non-equity, for example, lines of credit and factoring receivables.

The structure of the organization begins to be taken seriously and discussions are held about distinguishing the role of the corporate center from the role of the departments or business units. Issues about how the corporate center can continue to add value and avoid becoming cumbersome and bureaucratic are usually settled quickly in this stage. Policies are set forth, and the beginnings of corporate governance emerge after minor business-related disputes.

Here, for the first time, several critical aspects of organizational life begin to evolve. All of these aspects are of the "good news-bad news" variety. First, the *dominant logic* of the firm begins to take hold. This logic is the accepted methodology for assessing and solving problems and deciding on opportunities. Do executives make "gut level," back-of-the-envelope decisions, or do they have a penchant for analyzing certain kinds of data to support their decisions? The dominant logic also includes a preferred source of authority or a rank order of priorities in making decisions. Do customers have the definitive authority? Or do owners? How about the founders, with all their strengths and weaknesses? Or competitors, because of their strategic moves?

Also at this stage, the second aspect of organizational life—*its genetic code*—begins to be hard-wired into the firm's employees. The genetic code contains the values and core competencies required by the primary focus of the firm: innovation, service, or low cost. Strategy statements may include all three, but the firm's genetic code will revolve around just one, because trying to hedge all three would dilute focus and increase business risk.

The third thing that happens at this stage is the solidification of the overall strategy's *shape*—the right blend of speed, service, quality, cost, and innovation. While the genetic code centers on only one source of competitive advantage, the shape of the strategy is a mix of the dominant element plus influences from all the other issues the firm must consider in order to compete.

The good news in these three shifts in the organization is that they give everyone a pattern to follow. The pattern guides their thoughts and behavior and actually strengthens the culture by giving them a sense of belonging to a unique group. The bad news is that the pattern rejects *anything* foreign. This negative aspect is not noticed at this point, but will surface again in Stage 6, Revisioning and Wealth Creation. If the new business is a spin-off from an existing firm, additional bad news could arise in this and successive stages if leaders in the parent organization try to "paste" its dominant pattern and genetic code onto the more entrepreneurial venture. Every new organization should have the opportunity to form a dominant logic, pattern, and genetic code that arise naturally from its objectives and relationships. In fact, its leaders should actively resist replicating old patterns that may not be productive or beneficial at this stage of development.

Transition to Growth

Everyone in the organization is refreshed by the focus and control implemented in Stage 2, and they begin to see that controlled growth is possible within the pattern. The firm starts to find new ways of building on the success that has been created.

Stage 3: Growth

Strategic action in this stage may range from incremental growth to more explosive and chaotic change. It depends on the prudence and wisdom of the top management team—which may be a real team or a "confederation of feudal barons," as one client described it. The type of growth strategy also depends on how easy it is to identify and capture growth opportunities. Relative ease in this process can lead to an intoxicating drive for more and faster growth.

The typical strategic focus is toward moderate levels of growth and change. New products or extensions to products are either developed or acquired. Selling moves from merely taking orders to "value selling" or selling on features and benefits relative to the competition. An early form of customer relationship management is initiated, possibly intuitively, because key customer accounts are few and have grown with the firm. The move to regionalization or globalization is often part of this stage, especially if it means replicating the business, as Kinko's and many restaurant chains have done.

Perhaps the key aspect of this stage is the selection, development, and retention of people. While selection is still relatively informal, it is taken seriously. It is based on needed skills, but includes concern for a set of values, a certain "look" and priority in personal, family, and spiritual needs that are consistent with those of the leadership or "*dominant coalition.*" This is the group that, in the previous two stages, set by deed and example the dominant logic of the business, the shape of the strategy, the ubiquitous pattern, and the firm's genetic code. If there is an ample supply of talent in the market, new hires will be selected only if they closely match the dominant coalition. If the supply is short, people are hired with the hope that they will learn to conform to the "way" of the firm. Since total conformity almost never happens, the seeds are sown for confrontation in Stage 4.

As the business grows and is successful, heroes begin to be identified and held up as examples to others. Recognizing heroes can inspire the people of the firm, but it will also further ingrain the pattern, strategy shape, dominant logic, and genetic code that have been established.

Transition to Process Redesign and Improvement

The growth stage, like the vision and inspiration stage, is highly motivational and uplifting. But over-emphasizing the visibility of key "wins" and emergent heroes sets off the formation of power bases and inflated egos. These successes can also instill a cultural arrogance that says, "We know the right way," and hinders the emergence of new ideas and the challenging of dogma. The momentum of the growth stage is sometimes mistaken for real strategic leadership. Hard as it is to believe, disdain for the customer can actually occur in this stage, as customers have a way of spoiling the hero's ego rush in becoming a "legend." These counter-productive behaviors are the bad news of this stage and form the root cause of organizational silos and hubris in firms. Thus, they lead to Stage 4.

Stage 4: Process Redesign and Improvement

The reengineering revolution of the 1990s arose in response to the silo nature of companies and the growing arrogance that led executives to look "out" at the world through their corporate lenses, instead of "in" from the outside through the lens of the customer. Improvement efforts were structured in a number of ways, including:

- *Process reengineering:* developing line of sight to the customer, removing all non-value-added activity.

- *Six sigma quality:* striving for three parts per million defects or less and designing new products with customers and suppliers, perhaps connecting through an electronic town hall or portal capability.

- *Supply and value chain management:* creating systemic linkages from the customer back through the firm to all supplier and vendor relations.

- *Operational excellence and lean manufacturing:* employing mass customization, cycle time reduction, and all forms of just-in-time delivery and outsourcing of nonessential assembly.

- *Customer service:* offering ultimate levels of convenience and guarantee fulfillment, and gaining customer knowledge to improve service, sometimes before customers are even aware they have needs.

While not many firms have harvested all the possible benefits of the process revolution, most have seen moderate to dramatic improvement. We will not delve into the details of the revolution here, as they have been covered in great detail in the business literature. What is tantalizing to consider, however, is that the business cases and value propositions for these reengineering initiatives hide a growing conundrum.

How can a firm that considers the business case for any of these improvements possibly go wrong? The fact that many companies did go wrong, in spite of all the process improvements they made, begins the transition to Stage 5.

Transition to Product/Cost Optimization

In the face of competitive rivalry, an innate tension arises between the need for disruptive innovation to reinvent and transform a business and the unplanned shift in the dominant logic to a low-cost position—but not necessarily *the* low-cost position. A low-cost position is in one sense a safety net. It gives the firm the option of lowering prices, thereby quickly giving customers a perceived value relative to competitors that cannot lower their prices. A low-cost position allows a firm to maintain margins above planned safety net levels. This is the genius of Wal-Mart—"everyday low prices" does not mean the lowest prices; it allows the company to lower prices to retaliate against a competitor and still not go below planned margin levels or forego the growth of market value.

Given the ebb and flow of wins and defeats in the competitive cycle, the prime movers and process owners in a company *will almost always* tend toward a lower cost position unless management exerts concerted energy to stop it. Experience has shown that the strategy and drive to a lower cost position is, on balance, an easier road than the road to becoming a differentiator. It may take decades to build a differentiator advantage—as firms like Mercedes-Benz, Neiman Marcus, Godiva Chocolates, and others can attest. The firm that is an effective differentiator must plan and execute more disruptive innovations than the real low-cost provider if it is to maintain its form of current advantage.

Of course, if the firm intends to become *the absolute* low-cost producer in its competitive domain, as in the case of Wal-Mart, a move to the low-cost position becomes its dominant logic and shapes the entire strategy. But in many industries, not all players can or want to become the low-cost producer. Think of Rolls Royce and Lamborgini, for example. They have spent so many years building competencies as differentiators that they are now prevented from even thinking about lowering their cost positions. They may consider creating a separate brand for a low-cost/low-price offering, but the track record of companies with strong differentiation logics successfully spawning a low-cost/low-price subbrand has not been good. The slow, unperceived, and unplanned movement to a lower cost position puts the firm at risk in "no man's land," as it becomes neither *the* low-cost provider nor *the* pure differentiator.

Unless management takes determined steps to stop this unplanned migration, the firm aiming for a differentiated form of competitive advantage can find it has gutted any long-term commitment to real innovation. That commitment is essential to producing a pipeline of winning feature-oriented benefits and bold "burden-unloading" services that give customers differentiated value *and* the expectation of more to come. This continuing cycle of innovation is vexing for most firms, but it is necessary to ensure customers' loyalty and willingness to pay the premium prices that fund future innovation. As Michael Porter's seminal work reminds us, this unplanned migration does not give the drifting firm the key skills to become the low-cost provider either—and the firm gets stuck in the middle.[1]

The force to stop this unplanned migration to low-cost position is found in a set of executive processes that provide real commitment to funding and a demonstration of support for continual innovation. Without executive intervention, the operating processes of the firm cannot "lift themselves up by their own bootstraps" and shift to a dominant logic of innovation. Almost in every case, operating processes will gravitate to a dominant logic of cost efficiency and a central tendency with little variation. Expecting them to initiate the disruption of everything dear to them is simply too much to ask.

The next stage, Product/Cost Optimization, helps to correct this imbalance, but it is usually a frustrating stage and leads ultimately to Stage 6: Revisioning and Wealth Creation.

Stage 5: Product/Cost Optimization

This stage is a hectic search for the right blend of innovation and lower cost. For firms making the play to become the low-cost provider like Wal-Mart and many distribution-oriented firms, the goal is to perfect an enterprise-wide, lowest cost approach that cannot be duplicated by any competitor. For all other firms, it becomes a daunting balancing act of being a differentiator while establishing the lowest cost suitable for the desired level of differentiation. The fly in the ointment is how *real* the long-term commitment in funding will be for innovation through basic R&D and new product development. It is also a test of leadership courage to engage in repeated disruptive innovation as a start to reinventing the company.

Strategy documents may state one thing, but most R&D people will attest to the inconsistencies in their funding from one year to the next. The operational tension between the frequency of new service or product introduction and the drive to continue perfecting current products and services through greater efficiency and reduced cost is the same as the strategic tension between innovation and differentiation versus lower cost position. And, as was true in the previous stage, the solution is a set of executive processes that supplies "innovation energy" in the form of commitment to funding and visible, behavioral reinforcement.

The real rub is that there is no final right answer, nor will there ever be. Cycles of competition, innovation, customers' emerging needs, and internal barriers shape reality. The balance created between innovation and appropriate cost position will be right *only for an interim period.* In a matter of time, these two factors will be forced out of balance by external competition and the *internal barriers* that reinforce the tendencies of the dominant logic, dominant coalition, strategy shape, ubiquitous pattern, and genetic code. This is why static strategy categories such as differentiator vs. the low-cost provider and product leadership vs. operational excellence vs. customer intimacy cannot explain the reality that firms really struggle with. It is not that this focus in wrong, it is that there is a dynamic ebb and flow to organizational life. Things will be in balance for brief periods of time as they fit better with reality. Thus, management teams that are armed with the correct premises will be able to make earlier and better decisions than their rivals can.

Transition to Revisioning and Wealth Creation

At this point, the opinion leaders of the firm begin to sense that the very patterns, strategy, and culture set in the early days have become a liability and may need to be changed. In addition, some of the employees hired earlier in the hope that they would adopt the ways of the firm have not changed and have become instead a cadre of malcontents and under-performers.

Stage 6 is usually an all-out "war of change" to create a new pattern that is more inclusive. If the firm loses the battle, it will be acquired or go out of business.

Stage 6: Revisioning and Wealth Creation

This stage encompasses the search for a way to change or break the dominant elements of the organization to allow for survival or a next round of profitable growth. In the last 15 years, shareholder wealth—a framework that seeks to balance growth, investment, profitability, free cash flow, and risk—has been the rallying cry of boards of directors and visionary CEOs. This discipline has been used as an umbrella to launch and channel other initiatives typical of this stage.

In Stage 6 we begin to find answers to the critical questions that were raised in the previous stages. That is, who should bear the cost of the capital expenditure needed for differentiating innovation, and how should risk be managed? Can the dominant logic, coalition, and genetic code change and begin to accept diversity of all forms so the "pattern" can become more inclusive?

Shareholder wealth theories include the notion that the firm should apply external free market principles *inside the firm.* Units that contribute to increasing value are "keepers," and units that use up value are candidates for outsourcing or liquidation. It is helpful to broaden the notion of units and value to also include behavioral and attitude patterns that may need to change, as well. In this stage, therefore, the organization must try to optimize increasing customer value and customer satisfaction against the drivers of shareholder wealth.

This stage is usually a period of extreme initiative overload, which is curious because that actually increases business risk—one of the factors shareholder wealth is supposed to optimize. By this stage, however, the system has become so complex that no single mind can comprehend it all. To solve this problem, many firms attempt to create high performance teams, especially in top management. Executive processes come into scrutiny, and there are attempts to reengineer these processes, as was the case with operating processes in the process redesign stage.

The stage is characterized by an organization in a constant state of uneasiness and uncertainty. The pervasive concern is whether or not something so complex can really be improved.

Stage 7: Strengthening the Foundation for the Next Plateau

After two to four years in Stage 6, organizations seem to morph into this next stage, which combines the elements of both a final stage and a transition phase to a whole new cycle. If the Revisioning and Wealth Creation stage has produced new profitable growth, this period is for recharging batteries and thinking about the next plateau. When entirely new business ventures are launched, the firm enters the seven-stage cycle again. By re-entering Stage 1, the firm plants the seeds for its transformation or reinvention years down the road when it could become something totally different than it is today.

If the firm is unable to change the dominant elements of its organization, it becomes stuck or goes backward. Here, a major turnaround effort must be launched. If the firm survives in its current legal form, it may revert to a previous level of operations, but as a smaller unit after divesting some of its holdings.

THE IMPORTANCE OF INTEGRITY AND MAGNANIMITY

Strategies that focus on shareholder wealth work best when the overall economic climate is good. In a favorable environment, it is relatively easy, if a company's data are reliable, to identify and isolate business units that are "value destroyers." First, a required rate of return is established; then business units are measured against each other and against the norms of the market and industry peers. If, on the other hand, the economic climate is down, very few firms will be able to meet absolute levels of expected returns. In this case, rather than shifting the benchmark to match the best of the bad, we must find a better way to estimate strategic and operating health. That better way can be found in the continuous resolve of a company's leadership and employees to follow the seven stages of growth and continuous improvement with *integrity and magnanimity*.

The dictionary defines integrity as the firm adherence to a moral or artistic code; magnanimity implies a loftiness of spirit that enables one to bear trouble calmly, to disdain meanness and revenge, and to make sacrifices for worthy ends. While seldom invoked as critical behavioral skills in business, these complementary mindsets can offer guidance during uncertain times.

Following the path of integrity within the stages of growth and improvement requires the executive leadership to ensure that initiatives fit the particular stages in which they are launched and that initiative overload is avoided. As cycles of learning occur, the firm transitions naturally to the next stage of the process, and market value increases—the end measure of shareholder wealth. If internal or external events interrupt the process, the firm may have to go back to a previous stage, enter into a holding pattern at the current stage or create a hybrid stage by blending aspects from several stages.

In pure shareholder wealth terms, regression of this kind would call for a downgrade in the firm's stock price. However, because this move represents *integrity* within the logic and laws of the seven stages, and because the firm exhibits the magnanimity required, a step backward or standing in place is all that can be expected. Instead of signaling the replacement of current leadership, as may be called for by Wall Street analysts, these moves in a difficult environment should be viewed as key learning experiences that would be lost under new leadership.

There will always be cases in which the existing leadership should leave so that a new team can take over, but missing a couple of quarters of forecasts is not one of them. Instead, breaches of integrity and magnanimity should be the real consideration for changes in leadership. For example, there are times when operations should rule, as in Stage 4, Process Redesign. But if an ego-driven senior management team were to stand aloof from operations and assume credit for improved operational performance during this stage, integrity would certainly be lacking. Signs such as these are the real fundamentals for assessing a firm's strategic and operating health.

If you would like to measure the integrity and magnanimity in your firm throughout the seven stages, ask everyone the following questions:

1. Where is our company on its unique journey to growth and continuous improvement?

2. Do the company's key strategic initiatives fit with our stage on the journey?

3. Are we experiencing initiative overload?

4. Is the firm's market value growing?

5. Is the firm growing the value of its people? Is your personal value growing?

6. Does the firm experience continued cycles of learning as it progresses on its journey?

7. Is the leadership in the firm magnanimous when adversity strikes?

8. Do proposed initiatives give you the confidence that new, profitable growth will happen?

9. What is the likelihood of your staying with this company, assuming jobs outside the firm are plentiful?

If your company has an intranet system with a confidentiality feature, a poll of *all* employees on these questions could be conducted every six months. Trend lines would show movement from the first baseline measure. If the improvement does not meet the desired level, corrective steps could be taken.

The roadmap of the seven stages of growth and continuous improvement is a comprehensive and practical tool that can help a firm deal with the complexities of innovation, growth, and change. If the leadership of a firm can meet the integrity and magnanimity challenge, business can become "fun" again.

THE BENEFITS OF USING THE SEVEN STAGE ROADMAP

Certain kinds of initiatives are typically launched at each stage of the growth and improvement process. Figure 6.3 catalogs these initiatives according to their appropriate stages. The initiatives must fit their respective stages and be managed for cross impact. The leadership of the firm must prevent initiative overload, a prevalent problem in many firms today. Initiative overload causes many problems but the worst is that it inhibits root cause learning. Because of the clutter and confusion, people tend to work on symptoms instead of root causes, creating delays, stalls, and rework that obscure real learning.

It is equally important for the firm to move forward as quickly and prudently as possible in growing its market value. This rule holds true for publicly traded companies as well as privately held firms. Every step—the transition from one stage to the next, knowing when a firm needs to return to a previous stage, or launching new ventures that puts part of the firm back to Stage 1—must be led and managed with design, prudence, foresight, and speed.

The construct that includes the seven stages of growth and continuous improvement is a key delivery vehicle for traversing *a continuum of improvement phases* as the firm seeks to increase its market value. The 4Bs diagram shown in Figure 6.1 is a visual representation of this continuum. The cells in the diagram also represent options that contain:

- Differing degrees of innovation.

- Differing degrees of change management complexity.

- Choices depending on whether the firm seeks to be an industry leader or a follower.

- Choices that allow the firm to become a defining entity and "category killer."

If a firm is in the early stages of the process and/or if it lacks world-class execution prowess, initiatives will usually reside within the *Getting Better* quadrant of the 4Bs matrix. As the firm gains confidence from cycles of learning in execution, it will migrate toward the *Getting Bolder* quadrant in the upper right. *Unless a firm traverses the seven stages and moves quickly but carefully on a path from getting better to getting bolder, it will not grow in market value.*

In many cases, choosing strategic moves has become a piecemeal activity by individual executives, functions, or processes. This fragmented approach can be traced back to several factors. The first factor is the resistance of powerful line executives to centralizing information in any position other than the CEO, negating the possibility of leading strategy development and implementation from an enterprise-wide perspective. Attempts to install an improvement "czar," reengineering "king," or strategy development "guru" are resisted. Thus, if the CEO of a company is not a visionary architect, synthesizer, *and* implementer, piecemeal activity almost always follows.

The second factor is related to the reality that the average tenure of a CEO and his or her direct reports is about three years. On the other hand, the benefits from the corporate initiatives they have instituted may take years to be realized. Frequent changes in leadership can create a strategic approach that is linear, silo-ori-

Figure 6.3
Typical Initiatives in the Seven Stages of Growth and Continuous Improvement

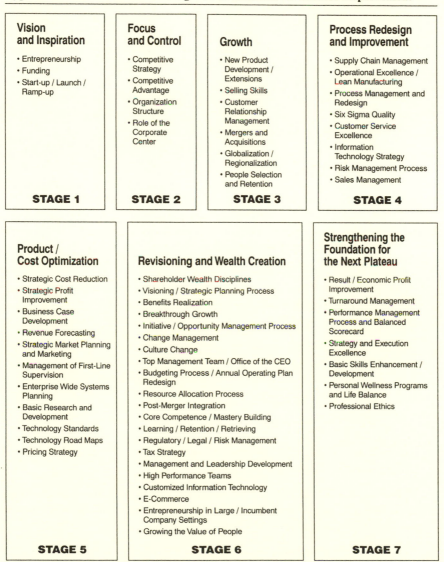

Vision and Inspiration

- Entrepreneurship
- Funding
- Start-up / Launch / Ramp-up

STAGE 1

Focus and Control

- Competitive Strategy
- Competitive Advantage
- Organization Structure
- Role of the Corporate Center

STAGE 2

Growth

- New Product Development / Extensions
- Selling Skills
- Customer Relationship Management
- Mergers and Acquisitions
- Globalization / Regionalization
- People Selection and Retention

STAGE 3

Process Redesign and Improvement

- Supply Chain Management
- Operational Excellence / Lean Manufacturing
- Process Management and Redesign
- Six Sigma Quality
- Customer Service Excellence
- Information Technology Strategy
- Risk Management Process
- Sales Management

STAGE 4

Product / Cost Optimization

- Strategic Cost Reduction
- Strategic Profit Improvement
- Business Case Development
- Revenue Forecasting
- Strategic Market Planning and Marketing
- Management of First-Line Supervision
- Enterprise Wide Systems Planning
- Basic Research and Development
- Technology Standards
- Technology Road Maps
- Pricing Strategy

STAGE 5

Revisioning and Wealth Creation

- Shareholder Wealth Disciplines
- Visioning / Strategic Planning Process
- Benefits Realization
- Breakthrough Growth
- Initiative / Opportunity Management Process
- Change Management
- Culture Change
- Top Management Team / Office of the CEO
- Budgeting Process / Annual Operating Plan Redesign
- Resource Allocation Process
- Post-Merger Integration
- Core Competence / Mastery Building
- Learning / Retention / Retrieving
- Regulatory / Legal / Risk Management
- Tax Strategy
- Management and Leadership Development
- High Performance Teams
- Customized Information Technology
- E-Commerce
- Entrepreneurship in Large / Incumbent Company Settings
- Growing the Value of People

STAGE 6

Strengthening the Foundation for the Next Plateau

- Result / Economic Profit Improvement
- Turnaround Management
- Performance Management Process and Balanced Scorecard
- Strategy and Execution Excellence
- Basic Skills Enhancement / Development
- Personal Wellness Programs and Life Balance
- Professional Ethics

STAGE 7

ented, and a serial pattern of single events. It is very difficult to achieve real cycles of learning within such a snapshot approach, and much critical learning can be lost. Real learning is gained only as the firm moves through all seven stages of the process and pursues all of the 4Bs of growth. Using the Initiative Management Process (Chapter 4) and the seven stages to traverse the 4Bs can mitigate the fragmentation these factors create.

The seven stages of growth and continuous improvement reinforce a leadership and management style that is dynamic, cyclical, cross-functional, and time bound. Although the New Science strives for the fastest practical cycle times, the gestation period for some initiatives may be five to ten years or longer. The snapshot view of time is, therefore, replaced with a continuous, motion-picture view. As the future becomes the present and as more clarity arises from root cause learning, the motion picture can be edited to create different endings (i.e., creating new strategies to ensure desired results). This is the essence of strategic management in the New Science—creating a desired future as opposed to being in a constant reactive mode. Firms that are building world-class strategy execution skills have the best chance of creating their desired futures.

Identifying the Barriers to Success

The transitions between the stages do not happen automatically. Barriers related to the firm's subject matter, process, structure, and culture may be encountered. These barriers must be identified, removed, and/or managed if the journey through the stages is to occur successfully.

- *Subject matter barriers* are created by a lack of knowledge required by a specific industry, product, or service. For example, if a company decides to produce a certain item, but does not have all the necessary technical knowledge, it would face a subject matter barrier.

- *Process barriers* include any impediment that causes longer cycle time or more rework and performing tasks that customers do not value and/or that make it difficult for them to do business with the company. All process barriers increase production cost and force prices up.

- *Structure barriers* interfere with customer interfaces. The company must reorganize to improve those interfaces. Structure is valuable because it groups like skills into a critical mass and helps to develop the *functional expertise* required for world-class execution. Maintaining the difficult balance between functional *excellence* and cross-functional *agility* is one of the key roles of structure.

- *Culture barriers* are the most difficult to identify and remove. They represent blind spots and faulty mental models, such as mistaking momentum for leadership and the inability to challenge one's own dogma.

If any one of these barriers is not identified, removed, and/or managed, progress through a stage or the transitions between stages will be blocked. When this happens, the firm will not create value for customers and wealth for shareholders at a rate and a degree of richness that would have been possible without the barriers.

Early Warning Signs of Barrier Presence

The following steps can provide warning signs of the existence of an organizational barrier.

1. Map the three categories of processes (executive, operational, supporting) to each class of barrier (subject matter, process, structure, culture). All classes of barriers can reside in any of the process types, however, nesting usually occurs as follows: (a) Executive processes contain structure and culture barriers; (b) Operating processes contain subject matter and process barriers; (c) Support processes contain subject matter, process, and structure barriers.

2. Measure cycle time, amount of rework, customer satisfaction, customer value, and cost for each key process within the three categories at the current or baseline time period.

3. Work with suppliers, vendors, and customers to establish ideal or desired measures.

4. Set a timeline for achieving the ideal measures.

5. Improve the metrics of cross-functional and cross-process teams to identify and drive out barriers.

6. Use link charts to show what actions are required to remove the barriers.

7. Use impact charts to show linkage to appropriate improvements for the firm, such as sales, margins, inventories, cash flow, turnover, stock price, and customer loyalty/retention.

8. Establish a culture of management activism and high performance teams that allow the necessary changes to happen.

This process creates a valuable role for the knowledge management function, which then becomes the keeper of root cause learning along the growth and continuous improvement journey.

CONCLUSION

This chapter has provided an extensive review of the seven stages an entity must go through in order to continue as a viable business. Each stage has good news and bad news contained within it. The bad news in one stage is a key factor in promoting the transition to the next stage. Could an intelligent and thoughtful management team lead and manage so that the bad news does not happen? Experience suggests not. A firm is fated to experience to some degree most of what is described in the seven-stage journey, because human nature—excitement, hope, desire for financial security, love, fear, greed, ego—all play a part. But the negative effects can be lessened if a management team is vigilant and watches for the signs of bad news in each stage.

Stage 7, Strengthening the Foundation for the Next Plateau, is described as the concluding stage or a stage that cycles back to Stage 1. However, in reality the activities of this stage can happen in the transition phase between any two stages. Where it will occur depends on the personal leadership style and philosophy of the senior executive team and how exhausting the previous stage was for the organization. If the firm needs to recharge its batteries after a successful but stressful stage, or if it needs to launch a turnaround action because of an unsuccessful stage, any of the typical initiatives from Stage 7 can be launched.

In the next chapter, we explore the dynamic laws of competition, how to describe a favorable and attractive external environment, the impact of environmental carrying capacity on competitive direction, and how to match four key competitive thrusts to dynamic environmental change—factors that are crucial for world-class strategy execution.

NOTE

1. Michael Porter, *Competitive Strategy: Techniques for Analyzing Industries and Competitors*, (New York: Free Press, 1980).

Chapter 7

The Dynamic Laws of Competition and Timing of Competitive Thrusts

The fourth aspect of world-class strategy execution is managing the dynamic laws of competition. To be effective, each of the four types of competitive thrusts—straightforward profitable growth, process improvement/reengineering, cost reduction, and turnaround management—must be correctly aligned with the realities of the external competitive environment.

So far, we have discussed:

- Foundation concepts for the New Science in Chapters 2 and 3.

- The key features of the Initiative Management Process in Chapter 4.

- The importance of executive, operating, and support processes being PALS with market rhythm in Chapter 5.

- And the stages of growth and continuous improvement in Chapter 6.

These topics provide a new way of thinking about strategy and execution and offer skills for improving internal management of related processes. The effectiveness of these processes depends primarily on the decisions and actions of a firm's executives. However, no business operates within a vacuum. There are myriad external factors that affect success or failure. In fact, the external environment *determines* the proper timing of all competitive efforts. In a sense, the external environment—to borrow from biology—selects *for* the thrusts that fit the best. Getting it wrong means disability or extinction. The dynamic laws of competition demand that a thrust be implemented in its most hospitable environment. Upsetting this natural fit with ill-timed competitive thrusts is a formula for headache or disaster.

A competitive thrust is an initial salvo at the very beginning of a shift in the favorableness of the external environment. If properly timed, the thrust allows the firm to be a first mover in this new environment. Nested within the thrust are initiatives that will flesh it out over time. By planning these thrusts to occur within the appropriate competitive environment, the firm guarantees the greatest probability of being successful in growing its market value. The business media have reported many ill-timed competitive thrusts over the years, proving that such mistakes are not unusual. For world-class strategy execution, the timing of competitive thrusts must be correct.

ASSESSING THE BUSINESS ENVIRONMENT

Four factors contribute to the actively changing conditions that surround a business: the competitive environment, the carrying capacity of the environment, the strategic and operational intricacy of the organization, and the complexity of technology required to compete.

Competitive Environment

The competitive environment can be assessed by estimating eight attributes: order, hostility, cost of entry, interconnectedness, extended community "policing" costs, turbulence and dynamism, fragmentation, and diversity.

- *Degree of Order.* This attribute is concerned with the degree to which industry firms act rationally, agree informally to their relative roles in the industry, and send legal market signals of strategic moves and advances through trade journals and industry publications.

- *Degree of Hostility.* This attribute considers the degree to which open price wars, marketing battles, and predatory moves and announcements have engulfed the industry.

- *Cost of Entry.* This important factor considers the cost required to enter a competitive space, whether that space is a narrowly defined industry or a more diverse "extended community" of suppliers, vendors, alliances, and otherwise "friendly" competitors.

- *Degree of Interconnectedness.* This measure is the degree to which an extended community of suppliers, alliance and joint venture partners, customers, and competitors have choreographed informal or contractual business relationships that are satisfactory to all parties.

- *Extended Community "Policing" Costs.* This attribute measures the cost of monitoring the quality and integrity of the community's members and applies only when there is a diverse, extended community of suppliers, alliances, vendors, and other competitors.

- *Degree of Turbulence and Dynamism.* Turbulence is measured by the extent of unpredicted variance around a growth trend line—the greater the unpredicted variance, the higher the turbulence. Dynamism refers to how frequently the unpredictable variance moves up or down over time.

- *Degree of Fragmentation.* This attribute considers how evenly divided market share is among many players. Its measure is the opposite of that found in highly concentrated industries in which only two or three competitors control the majority of market share.

- *Degree of Diversity.* This attribute describes the degree to which different forms of technology, product specification, branding style, and the like can successfully coexist.

Figure 7.1 describes the dynamic nature of these attributes. As the competitive environment changes, each of these attributes becomes more or less attractive for achieving profitable growth.

Figure 7.1
Attractiveness of Dynamic Attributes in the Competitive Environment

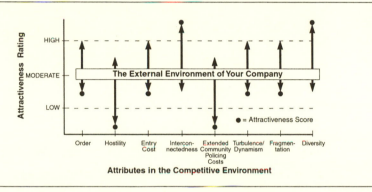

The most attractive environments for straightforward growth are those that are in the moderate range for the degrees of order, cost of entry, turbulence and dynamism, and fragmentation. In these attributes, the appropriate standing should be neither thoughtless conformity nor chaos. The desirability of low hostility and "policing" costs are readily apparent, while a high degree of interconnectedness is positive because an action or decision can have a rapid leveraged effect. However, there is a caveat on this point—if the community should begin to unravel, a high degree of interconnectedness could cause abrupt disruption and would require extreme vigilance on the part of individual participants. Finally, a highly diverse environment is attractive because it facilitates learning from others who have different dominant logics, patterns, strategy shapes, and genetic codes. Diversity also allows for trial and error. Gaining an early monopoly position, as Microsoft has, allows a firm the advantage of controlling diversity; however, this strategy takes years to develop and is inherently unstable. The most attractive attribute ratings are:

Attribute	*Rating*
- Degree of Order	- Moderate
- Degree of Hostility	- Low
- Cost of Entry	- Moderate
- Degree of Interconnectedness	- High (but risky)
- Extended Community Policing Costs	- Low
- Degree of Turbulence / Dynamism	- Moderate
- Degree of Fragmentation	- Moderate
- Degree of Diversity	- High

Carrying Capacity

The carrying capacity of the environment is a concept borrowed from biology. It seeks to measure how hospitable the environment is to a large, diverse "population" of firms. This factor is similar to, but different from, the diversity measure discussed above. Environments that have a high carrying capacity have enough customer demand—both actual and latent—to allow fairly large numbers of firms to coexist and thrive. A business environment with a high carrying capacity will also have the necessary input resources—land, labor, capital, and entrepreneurship—to fuel growth. Finally, this type of environment has a sufficient amount of capacity distributed among enough different players to ensure continuous innovation in the function and usefulness of products and services.

The concept of carrying capacity is much more inclusive than analysis of supply-demand balance in a competitive setting. A falling carrying capacity demands a move to a different thrust—quickly and ahead of the competition. Lingering and hoping for a return of the good life from earlier times is useless and foolhardy.

Scale, Scope, and Operational Complexity

Designing and building the growth of a company has the greatest chance of succeeding and creating shareholder wealth when the environment is favorable, the carrying capacity is high, and the firm is relatively small in scale, scope, and operational complexity. As time goes on and the firm grows and is profitable, it almost always becomes larger, broader in scope, and more complex, as well. Once competitors and others begin to take notice, they will move in with price reductions, marketing battles, and other tactical responses, even in the presence of barriers to entry. As competitive encroachment heats up, a technological leapfrog ensues or the cost of enforcing industry quality and integrity increases, and anxiety and uncertainty narrow the diversity of the industry as companies revert to the "tried and true." The end result is a less favorable environment for growth and a carrying capacity that will *always* fall (see Figure 7.2).

Technology

The competitive cycle can be affected by innovations in technology in all its forms—information technology, process technology, manufacturing technology, and the technology of product features. The impact of these technologies depends on the forces that are creating movement in the attributes of the competitive environment and the actions of the firm itself.

Some competitive spaces are highly dependent on technology as a condition of doing business. The aerospace, telecom, lighting, and computer industries are just a few examples of "high tech" endeavors. In other instances, such as small, cottage industries or mom-and-pop operations, the competitive space remains relatively "low tech," even though their products may be enhanced with information services and common carrier, overnight delivery.

Figure 7.2
Attributes of Company Status in the Competitive Environment

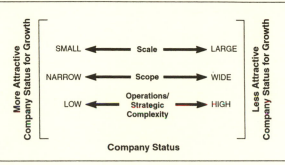

Some competitive spaces start off as low tech and evolve to high tech. For example, military weaponry has moved from a lower dependence on technology to a high tech stance, and the information, communication, and entertainment industries have converged in the form of wireless Personal Digital Assistants (PDAs). Sometimes an industry can reverse its direction and return to lower tech operations. In banking, for example, there was a movement away from ATMs, Internet banking, and other automated services as banks returned to providing services through real people. This direction seems to be reversing again as improved technology enables customization and personalized Internet services.

The impact of technology on the competitive cycle raises an important but difficult question. Most of the time, a move toward high tech will increase the carrying capacity of the environment. However, if a new technology introduces a higher standard, the carrying capacity of the environment can fall as the demand for the outmoded form of technology plummets and the firm that leapfrogged ahead does not have the productive capacity to fill growing demand. Demand may be present, but the capacity to deliver is lacking. The industry may rush to add capacity, but a shakeout could occur if customers become frustrated waiting for promises to be fulfilled.

In fact, the dynamics of technology's favorable or unfavorable impact on competition is uncertain and must be constantly assessed. The firm may choose to be a leader or a follower in technology, and in either case, it can achieve and practice world-class strategy execution skills and grow its market value. One of the next vistas for the New Science is observation and research to gain better knowledge of the timing and impact of technology as a crucial and ubiquitous variable.

FOUR TYPES OF COMPETITIVE THRUSTS

Categorizing the thrusts according to four types allows them to be calibrated and plotted against the external environment to ensure the most profitable results.

• Thrusts for *straightforward profitable growth* focus on incremental or breakthrough product/service extensions; product/service innovation; executive, operating, and support process innovation; reallocation of resources to improve processes that are customer priorities; disruptive technology launches; or tactical growth and profit improvement from price/cost optimizing. These thrusts are easier and more straightforward ways of achieving growth than the other thrust types, but they must be profitable from the standpoint of earnings and free cash flow.

• Thrusts for *process improvement or reengineering* are intended to improve or reshape executive, operating, or support processes in order to reduce cycle time, eliminate rework, and reduce cost associated with the value chain.

• Thrusts for *controllable cost reduction* are aimed at non-cost-of-goods-sold, non-direct-value-chain costs such as car fleet expense, cell phone charges, reimbursable expenses for travel or entertainment, real estate leases, and the use of outside resources.

• Thrusts for *turnaround management* are drastic measures that are employed to avoid bankruptcy. These thrusts require a combination of new strategic positioning and a radical return to basics in sales, cost, cash management, funding sources, and other functions.

TIMING COMPETITVE THRUSTS

As the competitive environment changes, the firm must move quickly to employ the appropriate thrust to ensure long-term wealth creation (see Figure 7.3). When the competitive environment is in its most attractive stage—carrying capacity is high, industry attributes are in their most favorable position, and the company is relatively small in size, scope, and complexity—profitable growth is easy and straightforward. As these factors change, that is, the carrying capacity starts to wane and the company has grown is size and scope, it becomes harder and harder to acquire profitable growth. The most important step then is to begin process reengineering to resynchronize processes and create a more efficient and effective organization. If the environment does not improve, the next step is to reduce costs that may have been overlooked in the reengineering phase. If the situation continues to deteriorate and competitive advantage is lost, it is time for turnaround action. When the turnaround is complete, the firm will come full circle as the environment becomes ready for a new round of growth. The firm has downscaled and is focusing on winning businesses and competencies; the environment is attractive once more (because losers have exited); and the carrying capacity is thereby increased, supporting a new series of thrusts for profitable growth.

With the exception of turnaround management—an option that must be pursued because it is the only way to save the company (as it was recently with Kmart)—the other competitive thrusts often suffer from suboptimal timing. Until now, there has been no tool to help calibrate a competitive thrust with a favorable environment. Improvement programs seem to be unleashed without any apparent reason or rationale. It appears that some of these seemingly irrational actions are the result of copycat behavior—a competitor announces its move for profitable growth, so other firms scramble to do the same. Or, a competitor installs an ERP package as part of a process improvement effort, so others jump on the ERP band-

Figure 7.3
Matching Strategic Thrusts to Company Status and the Carrying Capacity of the Competitive Environment

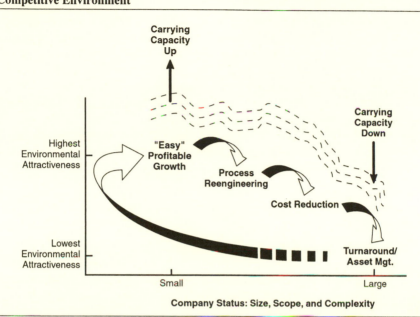

wagon. The lesson here is that *poor timing of competitive thrusts can ruin world-class strategy execution.*

There is a time—a "season," so to speak—that makes one of the four strategic thrusts more appropriate than the others. It is tantalizing to think that a firm could be in a continuous mode of profitable growth, but it cannot happen. There is an organic ebb and flow of competition that sometimes makes cost reduction the best option, and at other times favors process improvement. In fact, the dynamic laws of competition demonstrate that a "fall from growth" will always happen—the only question is when.

Turnaround management, if properly planned and carried out, can set the stage for a successive round of profitable growth. But a turnaround will be difficult for firms whose executives insist on making their mark with a growth option instead. It may be difficult for the typical "overachiever" type of CEO to wait for the right competitive environment before taking action. However, matching the competitive strategy with its appropriate environment lays the foundation for the successful execution of all strategies. Patience is an important virtue.

DO FIRMS HAVE A CHOICE?

Must the external environment always determine the choice of competitive thrust? Could not a powerful, "500-lb. gorilla" firm make the carrying capacity fall on its own timetable and advantage by cannibalizing its popular products? The answer is yes, it can, but the move is risky. Microsoft has worked this strategy successfully for years, but there are signs of end user dissatisfaction with too rapid introduction of product line extensions. The 500-lb. gorillas in the golf club manufacturing industry have not been as lucky. Callaway, Titleist, and TaylorMade have innovated club design so often that customers are furious. Golfers can buy a $500 club today and be told it is the ultimate instrument, only to find a newer and better version being released six months later. With an inefficient market for used clubs, golfers traded up for a while (and eventually found themselves with closets full of clubs and angry spouses), but they soon tired of the ploy. The whole industry is in a tailspin as a result.

Most firms are not 500-lb. gorillas, so the proactive cannibalizing strategy is not open to them. For these "mere mortals," the changes in carrying capacity and attractiveness of the external environment will continue to determine the choice of competitive thrust. Be right and be early should be the watchword.

CONCLUSION

The power of the dynamic laws of competition as an analytical tool is in its ability to provide early warning of changes in the competitive environment that signal a need to shift from one thrust to another. Inappropriately pouring the coals to growth in an inhospitable environment will almost always lead to problems, if not disaster. Applying this tool in making strategic decisions is crucial for the firm that seeks to achieve world-class strategy execution.

The dynamic and cyclical competitive environment outlined in this chapter underlies each of the seven stages of growth described in Chapter 6. As the firm seeks to grow its market value by using the seven stages to get better, broader, bigger, and bolder, it must successfully manage the inevitable cycles of change in the competitive environment. The ill effects of these cycles can be minimized if the firm's management team has developed a set of tools that allow it to turn the cyclical realities into a competitive advantage.

Once these tools have been mastered, the firms that want to go the last mile in gaining world-class strategy execution skill and prowess must consider the laws of ripple effects and interdependency—the last of the five aspects of world-class strategy execution. This final aspect is the focus of Chapter 8.

Chapter 8

The Laws of Ripple Effects and Change

This chapter presents the last of the five aspects that form the foundation of the New Science of Strategy Execution. The Laws of Ripple Effects and Change describe the broad causes and effects of every competitive and strategic move a company makes. These laws also address company-wide issues related to shifts in power and the struggle to maintain the status quo that may result from these moves. Understanding the laws will depend on how well you have absorbed the information in the previous chapters and how deeply you understand your firm and its people. While this chapter may have to be read more than once for its full meaning to be clear, it offers the possibility of making huge improvements in world-class strategy execution skills.

MANAGING RIPPLE EFFECTS

Most firms are highly complex—in structure, in decision-making responsibility, and in operational activity. This complexity makes it difficult for a top management team to be fully aware of the interconnectedness of various activities and the cross impact that change in one area may have on another.

The need for a tool to manage complicated organizations is based on six underlying premises:

1. No single person can fully understand the intricacies of an organization's life.

2. Major changes in the power, accountability, and decision-making processes of a company *always occur* when a firm traverses from one stage to another on the growth and continuous improvement journey (as discussed in Chapter 6) and implements one of the four competitive thrusts described in Chapter 7.

3. Honest mistakes will be made—it is not humanly possible to be right every time.

4. Powerful executives are strongly averse to admitting failure when they make mistakes.

5. When executives do not deal well with their mistakes, there is always fallout caused by shifts in power, accountability, and decision-making processes.

6. There is an order to the pattern of ripple effects that follow as a result of these events.

The Laws of Ripple Effects and Change begin with 11 interconnected modules of activity that describe a company's internal and external environment. While this may seem like a large number of modules, it represents the minimum number necessary to account for the changes in the strategic system. Fewer modules would reduce the explanatory power of the model; additional modules would make it too complex. The eleven modules are shown in Figure 8.1. Taken together, the model underlies a unique and powerful way of mapping and managing the "mega-burst" and "micro-burst" ripple effects of a decision made in one place and its consequences in other places.

Figure 8.1
The Eleven Modules of Business Performance That Are Affected by Ripples of Change

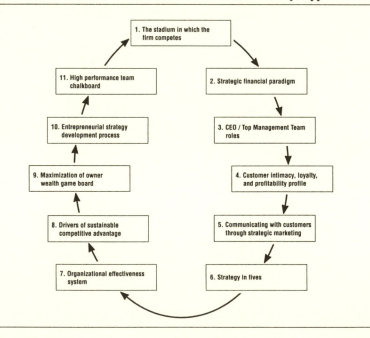

The ripple effects that occur in a complex system can cause severe disruption if they are not managed with foresight. Tracing the ripples provides an early warning of potential problems. Because there is a predictable order to shifts within the power, accountability, and decision-making processes of a firm, it is possible to track the effects of every type of change. Human behavior is also predictable, especially in the face of challenges and poor decisions. Using this tool can lessen the negative impact of an unplanned change, improve organizational learning, and help top management teams learn to gracefully accept their errors in judgment.

Understanding and mapping the ripple effects of change is often the missing ingredient in strategy execution. Vertical organization structures and compensation plans that encourage a culture of "not invented here" make it difficult for executives to become aware of the critical interdependencies that cause ever-broadening ripple effects. Even if a change is accompanied by obvious power struggles among key executives, it is easy to assume that the repercussions will be contained within the boundaries of a specific department or business unit—but they never are. And with the advent of corporate intranet systems, ripples now move more quickly through an organization. Even small changes can have large consequences within a very short time.

Appendix 2 details the types of decisions included in each of the modules shown in Figure 8.1, and provides a way of assessing where your company stands on each element. The results of your assessment will give you a baseline understanding of your current situation and how your organization is cross-wired for change. Appendix 3 contains a disguised, real-life client example. (The client was a business unit in a large aerospace corporation.) It shows the results of the unit's assessment at the baseline time period (T-0) and what the desired situation would look like five years hence (T-5). The desired situation was tempered with what executives thought would be the most likely evolution. They traced and extrapolated the ripple effects, and then made an honest assessment of what would really change. This business unit reported this exercise to be the most insightful, powerful, and honest look at the business ever taken. The law-like features of the ripple effects tend to temper overly enthusiastic attempts to create a "future state" that could never be achieved. The information in this chapter (and in Chapter 7) automatically restrains the amount of "stretch" an organization may reach for by showing what realistically can and will happen in the next three to five years, or whatever the time span is for its plan for the future.

THE ELEVEN MODULES OF BUSINESS PERFORMANCE

The clockwise order of the eleven modules in Figure 8.1 is deliberate. Many years of observation and experience have shown that the impact of strategic actions ripples through an organization in a certain way. Teams of executives in an SMU Executive MBA program used the approach in real company assessments, and every one of the companies reported being able to derive valuable insights and projected actions from the process. The approach is published here for the first time. We believe it has especially high potential for Master Builders, who can use it to top off their strategy execution skill set.

In Chapter 7, we discussed how changes in a key competitive thrust almost always starts with events in the external environment, which is represented here by Module 1–The Stadium. But the value of this paradigm is that change can start in any of the eleven modules, while the succeeding ripples will always fan out from there in a predictable way. Understanding these relationships allows the Master Builder to better plan for and manage key changes—a necessary ingredient for world-class strategy execution.

In the following section, each module is explained and its impact on a real, but disguised, real estate development company demonstrates the impact of change and its ripple effects.

1. *The Stadium in Which the Firm Competes.* The stadium represents that which is external to a firm's boundary and over which the firm has the least control. It includes *general influences*, such as political, economic, social, and cultural effects, and *industry specific influences*, such technology, competition, and customers. After the tax law change in 1986, the real estate development industry was in "free fall to disaster." This regulatory change had a negative effect on the finances of every development firm. As the underlying value of properties being used as collateral for loans fell to below the value of the loans, lenders began calling in developers' loans that were leveraged over many properties. As a result, real estate development came to a standstill. Some firms tried to expand into property management to stave off bankruptcy, but such a move was counter to their culture—property management was viewed as "second class" compared to the glamour of real estate development. The ripples touched every part of these organizations.

2. *The Strategic Financial Paradigm.* This paradigm derives from the financial sense of urgency that surrounds the top management team at all times. Executives in our hypothetical development firm found themselves engulfed in a situation characterized by a high burn rate of cash, failure to earn the required rate of return, and a high fixed-cost base. How should they respond? What changes should they implement?

3. *Top Management Team Roles.* Members of the top management team (TMT) must assume three crucial roles at all times—Architect, Master Builder, and Visionary. The Architect is the person who designs the organization's *form* , including structure, control systems, and information processes. The Master Builder is the one who blends together processes and people to achieve results. The Visionary is the executive with foresight and creativity who intuitively understands the trends underlying changes in customers' buying patterns and projects the impact of those shifts. Rarely will one person fill all three roles. Instead, team members with complementary styles take on these responsibilities. In our example, the chaotic situation tested top management teams in every development firm. Each firm needed a real leader and Master Builder to come forward. (The role of Architect was less important at this point because of the severity of the situation.) Inevitably, the chaotic situation began to have an effect on customers.

4. *Customer Intimacy, Loyalty, and Profitability Profile.* This profile represents the firm's true philosophy about the importance of providing superior value, satisfaction, and quality to ensure customer loyalty. This philosophy emerges most directly from the conditions in the first three modules. At the real estate development company, frustration was building over customer demands, and customer relationship processes were straining to maintain loyalty. One company executive was actually heard to say, "If it were not for these 'difficult' (actually a more colorful term was used) customers, we could have a good business again." This was definitely a sign that a new marketing approach was needed.

5. *Communicating with Customers Through Strategic Marketing.* This module asks whether or not a program is in place to provide individualized communications to distinct groups of customers. It also assesses whether or not a culture of true relationship management and consultative selling exists as a way of ensuring the loyalty and profitability of targeted customer groups. The developers discovered that they were in a marketing no man's land. They were sending mixed messages about the uniqueness of their evolving position, and they needed new media to pierce the noise in the marketplace. As things continued to deteriorate, people in the organization began to see the need for redefining the firm's mission and strategy.

6. *Strategy in Fives.* The top management team must now begin to organize strategic thinking and decision making around five interlocking aspects of strategy formulation: (1) grand strategy (purpose, vision, mission); (2) mission-level strategy (method of competition, desired leadership position, scale/critical mass, scope, cost structure and position, philosophy about the required rate of return, and the need and capacity for sharing among business units, functions, and departments; (3) action strategy (goals, objectives, initiatives, programs, projects); (4) reengineering (incremental or revolutionary change); and (5) key emerging topics, such as technology, changes in accounting standards, and regulatory challenges. These categories offer an effective way to communicate the strategic intent and direction of the firm to the rest of the organization. In the firm in our example, nervous executives overreacted and decided to "purge the culture and downsize, keeping only those people who 'get it,'" or, in other words, those who think like the executives themselves.

7. *Organizational Effectiveness System.* This module is the workhorse that houses a firm's total capabilities to deliver superior customer value, satisfaction, and quality and to sustain owner wealth. This system includes solutions to structure, processes, climate and culture, and recognition, reward, and people. The firm's "genetic code" is located in this module, and deep barriers can reside here. In our example, key development executives began to battle among themselves as they tried to reprogram the organization's genetic code and modify its culture to accept the changes that were necessary. As morale reached an all time low, people began leaving for opportunities elsewhere.

8. *Drivers of Sustainable Competitive Advantage.* This module reveals the root causes for a firm's current performance level. Drivers include marketing, new product processes, R&D, operating processes, people, structure, compensation, culture, information technology, total quality (six sigma), customer service, command of input resources, alliances and joint ventures, and total cycle time. Now the real estate development firm's operational capability was declining. People became disoriented and felt that the "ship was sinking." Shareholder/owner wealth was also threatened.

9. *Maximization of Shareholder/Owner Wealth Game Board.* All of the previous modules are evaluated in this module for their contribution to the firm's ability to earn more than its required rate of return. As income in the real estate firm declined, shareholders began clamoring for change. They wanted a renewed round of forecasting: How long was this situation going to last? Should the company go "back to basics" and employ its entrepreneurial skills to find a new way?

10. *Entrepreneurial Strategy Development Process*. This process is a comprehensive sys-
    tem that unites strategic thinking, strategic planning, and strategic decision making to
    support and synthesize all of the decisions, energy, and focus from the previous mod-
    ules. The process also lays a foundation that ensures that all the requirements necessary
    for successfully competing in the future are made available to the top management team
    and process champions in a timely, user friendly, and value-added manner. By pursuing
    these steps, the real estate development executives began an initiative to create high per-
    formance teams within the company.

11. *High Performance Team Chalkboard*. This last module allows the company to come to-
    gether as a team of high performance teams with focus, clarity, direction, energy, and
    leadership. It is the people catalyst for getting things done in the present and for starting
    new opportunity/initiative cycles for future performance. The leaders of the real estate
    organization created teams with surviving high potential employees and began to instill
    a high performance culture throughout the company.

The real estate development firm in the above example was affected by a
change in the tax laws—an external force for change. In hindsight, the change patterns and ripple effects they experienced came to be seen as fairly predictable. But
it did not seem that way to the executives who were dealing "in the moment" with
all that change. While the example portrayed an obviously difficult environment
and industry situation, it is important to remember that these ripple effects happen
even in favorable environmental and industry times as well. The energy and signals may seem to be weaker and the disruptions less minor, but as the dynamic
laws of competition explain, forces for adverse change are always building and the
undercurrents of change are there, nevertheless.

USING THE MODEL TO MAP CHANGE

This model demonstrates that the change created by ripple effects will occur in
predictable patterns. As a general rule, if a change is detected in one of the modules, it is sure to create a "mega-burst" of change *in the module directly following it
on the map*. It will then go on to create "micro-burst" changes *in the next four alter-
nating modules*. The hypothesis for these relationships emerged from years of
learning with a number of clients. Observations indicated that when a change of
sufficient importance happened, ripple effects would always emerge later in
unsuspected areas. After years of further analysis, a framework emerged, creating
a blueprint for monitoring and managing change (see Table 8.1).

The timing of ripple impact is an important factor in using the model as a predic-
tive tool. As a rule of thumb, a mega-burst impact will probably happen within one
to two market rhythms after the initial change is detected. For example, if key customers buy every three months, the market rhythm is three to four weeks, therefore,
a mega-burst change could be expected in three to six weeks, with the micro-burst
ripples following in three to five market rhythms or 15 weeks. A mega-burst change
is usually, but not always, stronger than the micro-burst ripples.

Table 8.1
A Blueprint for Change Patterns

MODULE OF FIRST CHANGE		MODULES OF RIPPLE EFFECT IMPACT
1. Stadium. Change pattern driven by environment.	*Mega-burst:* *Micro-bursts:*	2. Strategic Financial Paradigm 4. Customer Intimacy, Loyalty, and Profitability Profile 6. Strategy in Fives 8. Drivers of Sustainable Competitive Advantage 10. Entrepreneurial Strategy Development Process
2. Strategic Financial Paradigm. Change pattern driven by financial risk exposure.	*Mega-burst:* *Micro-bursts:*	3. Top Management Team Roles 5. Winning through Strategic Marketing 7. Organizational Effectiveness System 9. Owner Wealth Game Board 11. High Performance Team Chalkboard
3. Top Management Team Roles. Change pattern driven by leadership.	*Mega-burst:* *Micro-bursts:*	4. Customer Intimacy, Loyalty, and Profitability Profile 6. Strategy in Fives 8. Drivers of Sustainable Competitive Advantage 10. Entrepreneurial Strategy Development Process 1. Stadium
4. Customer Intimacy, Loyalty, and Profitability Profile. Change pattern driven by customers' dissatisfaction.	*Mega-burst:* *Micro-bursts:*	5. Winning through Strategic Marketing 7. Organizational Effectiveness System 9. Owner Wealth Game Board 11. High Performance Team Chalkboard 2. Strategic Financial Paradigm
5. Communicating and Winning through Strategic Marketing. Change pattern driven by miscommunication with the customer.	*Mega-burst:* *Micro-bursts:*	6. Strategy in Fives 8. Drivers of Sustainable Competitive Advantage 10. Entrepreneurial Strategy Development Process 1. Stadium 3. Top Management Team Roles
6. Strategy in Fives. Change pattern driven by change in grand strategy.	*Mega-burst:* *Micro-bursts:*	7. Organizational Effectiveness System 9. Owner Wealth Game Board 11. High Performance Team Chalkboard 2. Strategic Financial Paradigm 4. Customer Intimacy, Loyalty, and Profitability Profile

A Blueprint for Change Patterns

MODULE OF FIRST CHANGE		MODULES OF RIPPLE EFFECT IMPACT
7. Organizational Effectiveness System. Change pattern driven by reprogramming the genetic code.	*Mega-burst:* *Micro-bursts:*	8. Drivers of Sustainable Competitive Advantage 10. Entrepreneurial Strategy Development Process 1. Stadium 3. Top Management Team Roles 5. Winning through Strategic Marketing
8. Drivers of Sustainable Competitive Advantage. Change pattern driven by desire for world-class status / leveraging all resources.	*Mega-burst:* *Micro-bursts:*	9. Owner Wealth Game Board 11. High Performance Team Chalkboard 2. Strategic Financial Paradigm 4. Customer Intimacy, Loyalty, and Profitability Profile 6. Strategy in Fives
9. Owner Wealth Game Board. Change pattern driven by owner wealth requirement.	*Mega-burst:* *Micro-bursts:*	10. Entrepreneurial Strategy Development Process 1. Stadium 3. Top Management Team Roles 5. Winning through Strategic Marketing 7. Organizational Effectiveness System
10. Entrepreneurial Strategy Development Process. Change pattern driven by desire for industry foresight / entrepreneurship.	*Mega-burst:* *Micro-bursts:*	11. High Performance Team Chalkboard 2. Strategic Financial Paradigm 4. Customer Intimacy, Loyalty, and Profitability Profile 6. Strategy in Fives 8. Drivers of Sustainable Competitive Advantage
11. High Performance Team Chalkboard. Change pattern driven by desire for action / execution.	*Mega-burst:* *Micro-bursts:*	1. Stadium 3. Top Management Team Roles 5. Winning through Strategic Marketing 7. Organizational Effectiveness System 9. Owner Wealth Game Board

This powerful tool gives business leaders an early warning signal and allows them to manage the bursts of change as soon as a shift is detected in any of the modules. Whether the first change is initiated internally or externally, executives can apply this foresight to take appropriate measures in the modules of potential impact.

Some firms will find themselves in a situation where important change is happening in all the modules at the same time. In this case, every change will unleash its own mega- and micro-bursts, creating multiple problems to be addressed. While some top management teams have become dysfunctional under circumstances like this, it is possible to record the changes, module by module, and then rank them in terms of impact and importance. Used in this way, the tool allows for managing massive change.

Finally, this approach and tool can be used for dynamic strategic planning, as described in the case study in Appendix 3. The baseline assessment (at T-0) measured the market rhythm of the case-study firm as follows:

- High ticket purchases by their best customers occurred about once every 18 months in this business-to-business situation. The rule of four to five times as fast yields a market rhythm of 4.5 months.

- Service purchases and upgrades were purchased about once a year, creating a market rhythm of about three months.

- Averaging the two estimates, and weighting toward the service rhythm, revealed an average market rhythm of 3.5 months.

Armed with this information, strategists debated between what they wanted the future to look like in five years (T-5), and what they thought could happen realistically given the impact and timing of key ripple effects. It was interesting to watch as powerful executives created a desired future using a tool that allowed them to unearth process and culture barriers that could block movement from T-0 to T-5. At some points, they looked at each other and said, "*We are the problem.*" Because this was an engineering culture, this rigorous approach allowed soft culture change to begin obliquely in a culture that had resisted conventional change management techniques.

CONCLUSION

Following the Laws of Ripple Effects and Change can guide a firm in improving its current performance and in fulfilling its long-term potential. A member of the top management team must take on the Master Builder's role and create a blueprint that will lessen the effects of inevitable change. This approach can greatly aid dynamic strategic planning by helping firms move from the current time to a future time in a way that blends "stretch" with reality. Seeing the components of change and understanding the challenges of change encourages people to accept moving forward to an uncertain future instead of staying within the status quo. These steps are absolutely indispensable for accomplishing world-class strategy execution.

WORLD-CLASS STRATEGY EXECUTION: A SUMMARY CASE STUDY

Before launching into Part III of the book, it may be useful to take a brief look at how the five aspects of the New Science work together in practice. This is a case study of actual events, although the company involved has been disguised. The author led strategy development, execution, and growth efforts for this company for four years as an outside resource, but was regarded as a member of the top management team during the entire time.

A leading manufacturer of products for the do-it-yourself homeowner, for example, hand tools, caulk, mailboxes, weather stripping, and the metal strips used in laying carpet, had organized fluid, strategic market units (SMU) that overlaid an organization of product divisions and geographic units. The SMU responsible for weather stripping had come under intense competitive threat, and a stretch goal was set to grow revenue and profits by 15 percent within one year. This SMU sold to the "big box," power retailers like Home Depot, Lowe's, and Builders Square and to independent hardware stores. At a strategy summit meeting, a critical, "bet-the-company" decision was made to focus on the independents and to dominate that space. The independents were willing to pay premium prices because they needed specialized, fast-order, less-than-full-truckload, and online customer service capabilities, which gave the SMU higher margins. The challenge was to grow revenue and increase profit by 15 percent while focusing on this space.

During the previous three years, this SMU had undergone process reengineering and product/cost optimization. It was now in the revisioning and wealth creation stage detailed in Chapter 6. Using the axes on the Strategy Execution Grids shown in Figures 3.1 and 3.2 as thought-starters, the SMU team discussed how more pure, quality-in-use value could be added to the product, while costs-per-unit-sold were lowered and market rhythm capture increased. The fact that the company held the original patent on weather stripping allowed the team to build on this strength. After two weeks of experimenting, the team hit on a simple but brilliant solution. Color-coded packages of weather stripping would be mounted on a large, cork pegboard. One color would be for doors, one for windows, one for automobiles, another for plumbing uses. The cork pegboards would be mounted on a wall in all independent hardware stores so customers could see the various uses and benefits of weather stripping. The descriptions on the color-coded packages were "on-the-job-training" for salespeople, which lowered training costs and cycle time for the stores. With every changing season, the package types could be rearranged for emphasis, thus potentially capturing more market rhythms.

At the time, the shape of this strategy (speed, service, quality, cost, and innovation) surpassed competitors and caught them off guard. Strategic planning, resource allocation, budgeting, supply-chain, customer-service, and ERP processes were all made PALS with the market rhythm—which was three to four weeks. The various process owners became supportive of launching this initiative, and it proceeded successfully after a brief period of managing change using the eleven modules of business performance described in Chapter 8 as a guide. The initiative became a growth initiative (in a fairly slow-growth industry), so it seemed appropriate to put into place a central oversight committee to work according to the principles set out in Chapter 4. The SMU initiative team also worked with the owners of executive, operating, and support processes in a fluid, top-down and bottom-up information flow. The initiative team identified and removed subject matter, process, structure, and culture barriers throughout the firm that could slow the initiative's progress; and they followed the Law of Ripple Effects and Change (Chapter 8) to manage cross-process and cross-geographic ripple effects inside the firm and competitor-driven ripple effects in the environment. At a critical point in the journey of this initiative, it was declared a "Go Initiative," which meant it now had board-level visibility and was expected to directly increase the market value of the firm. The SMU realized it now had to deliver and mustered many of the attributes of a high performance team, which are defined in Chapter 9.

Revenue in this SMU went up 30 percent and profits grew by 20 percent within nine months. The attributes of this successful lightning strike—simplicity, modularity, high value-in-use, combined with lowered costs and seasonal package changes for more market rhythm capture—were quickly copied by the other SMUs for use in their various product lines. They were able to select what was appropriate for their specific product lines and to add nuances and new learning at a very fast pace. These SMUs also customized the five strategy execution aspects to meet their unique competitive requirements. They did not, however, change the basic integrity and content of the five aspects and their linkages so that a common learning base could be maintained.

While this success story could be explained by a combination of other management approaches—six sigma quality, high performance teams, intrapreneuring, reengineering, shareholder wealth discipline, and so forth—the five aspects of the New Science of Strategy Execution gather them all into a more inclusive, unified methodology. In the end, results are achieved through cycle time reduction, rework elimination, and cost reduction in the *entire suite* of executive, operating, and support processes. At a strategic and operating level, these practices improve most of the classic drivers of shareholder wealth. Because the New Science lays out a growth, innovation, and continuous improvement roadmap that builds a platform of success and confidence, bigger, broader, and bolder initiatives can be added, thus managing risk. The grittiness of execution can now marry the boardroom mandate for increasing wealth in a way that gets things done.

PART III

PROGRAM MANAGEMENT AND MEASUREMENT

Chapter 9

Putting It All Together to Drive Market Value

The discussion in this chapter assumes that a company is using all five of the aspects of the New Science of Strategy Execution. These aspects were presented separately in the previous chapters so a firm can work to adopt them one at a time, adding new skills as the organization's confidence and success in strategy execution grows. Good project management in an initiative management process (Aspect 1) moves a firm about 30 to 40 percent of the way to world-class status. The other four aspects—making executive, operating, and support processes PALS with market rhythms (Aspect 2), mapping the innovation and growth journey (Aspect 3), the dynamic laws of competition (Aspect 4), and the laws of ripple effects and change (Aspect 5)—build cumulatively until the firm nears the 90 percent mark. Methods for achieving the remaining 10 percent will undoubtedly emerge in the future. As our knowledge about world-class strategy execution grows, practitioners and theorists are continuously developing new skills and tools to enhance strategy execution success.

In this chapter, we describe the guidance, management, and leadership required to bring the five aspects together to create a fast, sleek wealth creating firm. For large, established firms, it may mean rethinking the organization; for smaller firms and new ventures, it may provide a blueprint for organizing from the start.

HIGH PERFORMANCE TEAMS DEFINED

To successfully unite the five aspects of strategy execution, the firm must conceive of, plan for, and then establish high performance teams. These teams provide the structural basis for world-class strategy execution. High performance teams must possess certain attributes, which include:

- Participative leadership *combined with* assertiveness and accountability by the team's "prime mover."

- Shared responsibility and a division of labor based on individual strengths.

- Alignment on a sole purpose that is real and important.

- Communication that is both supportive *and* direct, depending on the situation.

- The ability to say "no," while sustaining motivation.

- Focusing simultaneously on the present and the future.

- Focusing on priority tasks while holding others in backlog.

- A field of vision broader than the immediate task.

- Being alert to and prepared for the unforeseen.

- Creative talents.

- Rapid response.

Creating and reinforcing these attributes has helped many companies to successfully establish high performance teams. A simple diagnostic instrument based on the above attributes can be used to assess the status of any team. Achieving a 5 on a 1–5 scale for each attribute would indicate world-class status. Wherever there is a gap between the present assessment and a world-class score, corrective training and development can be employed.

THREE TIERS OF HIGH PERFORMANCE TEAMS

World-class strategy execution requires three tiers of high performance teams:

1. The Program Office Team

2. "Powers-of-Three" Initiative Oversight Teams

3. Initiative Teams

The Program Office Team

The program office structure and culture allows productive executive action to replace acrimonious infighting and politicking. This team is chartered to oversee the search for root causes of performance results within the entire strategy execution system. Figure 9.1 shows how the program office is organized. The high performance team that makes up the office is responsible for launching all aspects of strategy execution through the initiative teams. The office would use the initiative management process to define its activities. It would drive all actions to completion through cross-functional initiative teams (CFT) and remove barriers using specially trained and chartered barrier removal teams (BRT). The office itself would be responsible for mediating any conflicts that cannot be resolved within these working groups.

Figure 9.1
Strategy Execution Program Office Structure

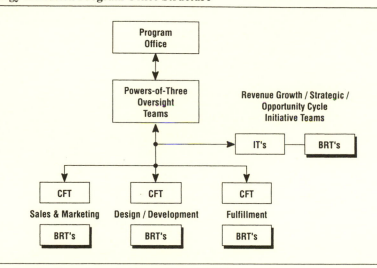

Source: Based on discussion at the Thomas Group in 1998.

The program office must be formed and chartered for oversight and commitment to drive all the New Science efforts to planned results with agreed-upon cycle times, little or no rework, and planned cost parameters. The name of this office should reflect the firm and its culture. For example, it may be called the Business Improvement Team (BIT), the World-Class Execution Team (WCET), or the Results Improvement Team (RIT). The possibilities are endless.

The process architecture for the program office is shown in Figure 9.2. This process is the blueprint for driving all strategy execution efforts to yield measurable business results and to capture valuable single and double loop learning along the way. The architecture blueprint should be replicated in all strategy execution teams.

A high performance team culture can take root throughout the organization if the program office team can *effectively* communicate that the barriers causing lengthy cycle times, rework, and cost overruns are a common enemy to world-class strategy execution and wealth creation.

"Powers-of-Three" Initiative Oversight Teams

The second tier of high performance teams is made up of oversight teams for categories of key initiatives. These categories will consist of groups of initiatives based on the 4Bs matrix and the seven stages of growth and continuous improvement. For example, all initiatives related to expanding customer platforms (getting broader) would receive oversight from the same powers-of-three team.

Figure 9.2
Program Architecture for High Performance Teams

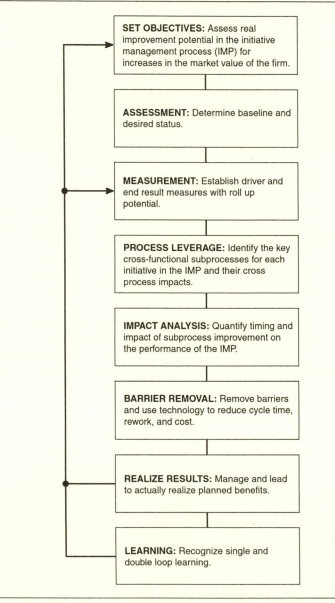

SET OBJECTIVES: Assess real improvement potential in the initiative management process (IMP) for increases in the market value of the firm.

ASSESSMENT: Determine baseline and desired status.

MEASUREMENT: Establish driver and end result measures with roll up potential.

PROCESS LEVERAGE: Identify the key cross-functional subprocesses for each initiative in the IMP and their cross process impacts.

IMPACT ANALYSIS: Quantify timing and impact of subprocess improvement on the performance of the IMP.

BARRIER REMOVAL: Remove barriers and use technology to reduce cycle time, rework, and cost.

REALIZE RESULTS: Manage and lead to actually realize planned benefits.

LEARNING: Recognize single and double loop learning.

Source: Contains a Thomas Group methodology and is reprinted with permission.

These teams must contain at least three executives. Studies have shown that a work group must have a minimum of three people in order to maintain the necessary checks and balances. The various oversight teams should be composed of people with unlike backgrounds, differing dominant skills, and varying viewpoints so potential blind spots can be overcome through healthy disagreement, constructive conflict, and positive activism. The power of three is a tool that tries to offset the negative effects of an organization's dominant coalition, dominant logic, and established genetic code, and its current shape of strategy.

Key individuals may be members of both the program office team and one of the powers-of-three oversight teams, depending on the needs of the firm. Assigning people to single or double team participation, however, will require finding a way to fund their release from their daily responsibilities. (Sometimes money can be found in the business case for process redesign and improvement.) The New Science of Strategy Execution will not work unless these adjustments are made. The main organizing principle in any company structure should be its initiatives, its initiative management process, and its initiative teams. If the program office hedges or waffles in any way on these imperatives, the New Science will become just another management fad.

Initiative Teams

The initiative teams are formed in the initiative management process as discussed in Chapter 4. We mention them again here because they now have interlocking relationships with a powers-of-three oversight team and the program office team. Initiative teams are cross-functional and serve to lead, manage, and push their initiatives through the initiative management process.

This is a very practical way to make the New Science of Strategy Execution work. The foundation of successful execution is putting winning initiatives into play as quickly and prudently as possible and managing these initiatives at world-class cycle times and yields. Initiative teams must have the visibility and power equivalent to the routine functions of the firm.

It is at this rich level of leadership and management that checks against the 10 S's must be made. (For a review of the 10-S model, see Chapter 3.) In its original business case, an initiative is expected to support all 10 S's unless the program office grants an exception. However, as it travels through the three gates and four phases of the process and as competition heightens, an initiative can lose synchronicity with one or more of the 10 S's, such as speed, simplicity, and self-confidence. These concerns must be raised with the appropriate powers-of-three team and/or the program office team as soon as they are perceived. In practice, the 10 S's become a beacon, guiding the initiative teams through the stormy seas of change, confusion, clutter, and fatigue.

MEASURING PROGRESS: THE REAL CATALYST FOR CHANGE

Measurement is the key to achieving results through the strategy execution system. Those who work on the shop floor know the value of driver and outcome measures in documenting manufacturing cycle times, process yields, scrap quantities, and so forth. The entire strategy execution system of executive, operating, and support processes must gain significant value from these measures as well. Driver measures are the root causes of performance and are *leading* indicators of potential results. Three driver measures are sufficient: the cycle time of the process, the first-pass yield (FPY) of the process (that is, the percent of intended results achieved without rework), and the cost of the process. *Lagging* measures deal with end results. They are familiar measures such as sales growth rate, margin growth rate, and stock price growth. Customer satisfaction can be used as either a lead or lag measure or both, depending on how it is measured. For example, measuring the percentage fill rate correct the first time is a proxy for customer satisfaction, and as such would be a leading measure. Measuring how likely customers are to switch to another vendor—more of a loyalty measure—would be lagging measure.

In strategy work, it is important to measure the drivers of all executive processes. Many times a CEO will have moved on to other assignments before the real end results are posted, therefore, it is useful to install an early warning system that measures the means to the results. "Cockpit charts" or "dashboard displays" can be used to portray customized measures for executive process drivers and results measures, just as they are often used for operating and support processes. A cockpit chart can be developed for all functions, processes, initiatives, and business units. These charts can then be rolled up into a single corporate metric for the powers-of-three teams and the program office team. Figure 9.3 contains an example of a cockpit chart of the key drivers and results of a firm.

As a general rule, critical work on driver measures must be completed during the first half of the project so that the major executive processes can be PALS with the operating and support processes and with market rhythms. Once driver measures have been institutionalized, the direct work of producing results can become the focus of the second half of the project's life.

The following rule of thumb can be used to estimate the duration of a major project such as a reengineering effort or a group of initiatives that support the launch of a new business:

- For firms with a billion dollars in revenue and market rhythms of *more than one month*, the time between making the necessary improvements in the drivers and realizing end results is 25 to 30 times the rhythm of the marketplace. For example, if major customers buy every four months, the market rhythm would be about four weeks (1/4 of the buying cycle). The total project time would be about 100 to 120 weeks or 25 to 30 months.

- Firms with more than a billion dollars in revenue will take 15 to 25 percent longer.

- For firms with market rhythms of *less than one month*, the formula is less reliable.

It will take at least a year to engrain the culture of the New Science within an organization. It takes time for the project to be structured, for the three tiers of high performance teams to be formed and trained, and for work to begin. It also takes time to gain small wins around which people can celebrate and develop a culture of success. The process requires changing behavior, which is a relatively slow process, especially in adults. Forcing change too quickly can be self-defeating.

Figure 9.3
"Cockpit Chart" of Competitiveness Indices

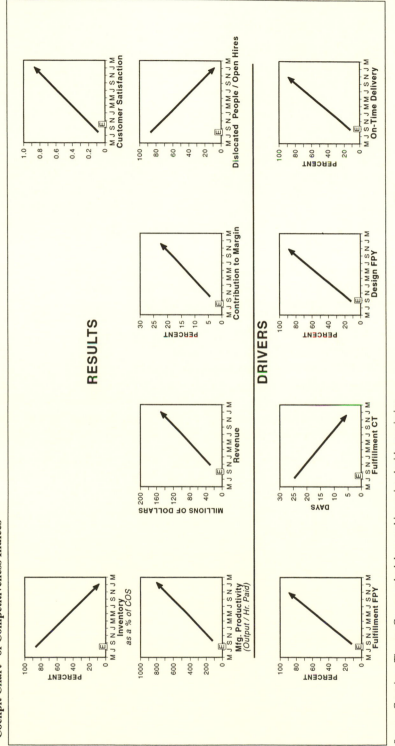

Source: Contains a Thomas Group methodology and is reprinted with permission.

SINGLE AND DOUBLE LOOP LEARNING

As soon as a platform of confidence and success has been established, the three tiers of teams are poised to gain both single and double loop learning—one of the greatest benefits of the New Science system. Single loop learning is achieved by comparing the actual performance of a given strategy with its desired or expected performance. If there is a gap, the strategy is changed to close the gap. Double loop learning goes beyond the analysis of results to identify the mental models that *gave rise to the strategies in the first place*. It is, of course, another way of lessening the negative aspects of the dominant coalition, logic, pattern, strategy shape, and genetic code and improving the approach so that similar mistakes are not made in the future.

As teams improve and benefits become visible, a continuous analysis can be applied using a database of all single loop variances. The following approach to this analysis may be useful:

- A computer program containing an "intelligent" algorithm can search the data for root causes and effects and then portray a series of dynamic models that represent how the three tiers of strategy execution teams are working.

- Frequent and severe single loop variances are almost always rooted in faulty mental models, blind spots, team dysfunction, and/or individual inertia in strategy development and execution.

- The models can be examined for frequency, location within the firm (a particular unit, process, function, or geographic area), and severity of the variances. More useful models can be continuously constructed and tested, and change management can adopt the new behaviors that are required.

The real value of this approach, if enabled with appropriate technology, is that it can occur continuously in real time, and double and single loop violations can be automatically sent to the three tiers of strategy execution teams.

CONCLUSION

The three tiers of strategy execution teams will not become bureaucratic if the 10 S's are championed and used to drive performance excellence. The power and benefits of the New Science of Strategy Execution are real, and firms are beginning to use it as a way of leveraging prior investment in processes, leadership, and wealth creation. In the next chapter, we take a step back and discuss the source of new ideas for product line innovation.

Chapter 10

The New Science and Product Line Innovation

The remarks in the previous chapters assumed that firms have an adequate approach to finding or conceiving of new products and services to feed into the initiative management process. It was also assumed that approved initiatives were adequate to meet world-class requirements of a particular stage of growth, whether pursuing one or more of the 4Bs—getting bigger, better, broader, or bolder—or focusing on one of the four competitive thrusts—profitable growth, process redesign, cost reduction, or turnaround—as described in Chapter 7. In fact, even though Phase 1 of the initiative management process is titled Scenario Generation, its emphasis is not on creating a new initiative but on generating information, energy, and a business case to propel a *known* initiative forward.

Working toward world-class strategy execution status helps to remove clutter and confusion so that innovation processes are improved. In this chapter, we will consider a way in which firms can refine their processes for creating new products and services that are either line extensions or totally new to the market.

There is a vast literature available on innovation and the commercialization of innovative ideas. We will not repeat those ideas. We will instead address a process of product line innovation that is consistent with all aspects of the New Science of Strategy Execution.

The development and launch of new products and services, that is, innovation, is at the root of successful wealth creation. Creativity is an individual's cognitive and intuitive ability to bring forth novel and unique ideas by connecting formerly unconnected strands into a totally new pattern. Innovation, on the other hand, is the translation of that creative spark into a product or service that customers will want to buy in order to satisfy an apparent or latent need.

The product line innovation process we present here is based on the following premises:

- Creativity must be processed to emerge as innovation.

- Innovation must pass through a process to emerge as a priority initiative that receives funding and commitment.

- The prioritized initiative(s) must go through a process that allows critical input from all executive, operating, and support process owners; identifies and removes barriers; and attaches metrics for cycle time, rework, customer satisfaction and value, cost, and financial realization—that is, the initiative management process.

An innovation does not have to reach breakthrough status to contribute to wealth creation. If the product line innovation process is working well, an innovation that produces a better product or service is sufficient at least 80 percent of the time. While they cannot be predicted, inspirations for breakthrough concepts are more likely to happen if the product line innovation process is installed. The persistent drive to seek better products and services often "knocks on the door" of breakthrough ideas.

THE PRODUCT LINE INNOVATION PROCESS

Before we begin a discussion of product line innovation, we must differentiate between it and new product design and development.

New product design and development involves determining a product's features to meet known needs and balancing its cost with what a customer is willing to pay. Recent advances in information technology allow a firm, its suppliers, vendors, and customers to work together on these issues. Most design/development processes are really variations of the initiative management process (IMP). The IMP is an overarching process that manages *all* initiatives that are generated from a variety of executive processes. A design and development process could be *one* of those initiatives.

The process of *new product line innovation* is very different. This process tries to extract the resident creativity in a firm to *generate totally new product and service ideas that will be eventual winners*. These new ideas may be line extensions or entirely new concepts. A process for product line innovation puts order and structure around the time when ideas are percolating and emerging. If the idea gets beyond the "thought in the shower" stage, sorting out and experimentation may last for years, and the tasks that should be undertaken may involve huge amounts of rework, stalls, and restarts. Imposing a structure of cycle times on this period makes the "found" initiatives as easy to develop as any other.

The New Science approach to innovation puts structure and measures into the firm's activities before the actual design and development process begins. Figure 10.1 shows the interconnected steps in the complete process of developing *product line* innovation. New *product* design and development is only one step in the process (Step 6 in Figure 10.1).

It is important to note here that the people in the innovation units of most firms will resist the imposition of process metrics and discipline. They will disparage these efforts based on their belief that the creative process should have no boundaries and attempts to measure it like an operating or executive process will reduce

Figure 10.1
The New Science Product Line Innovation Process

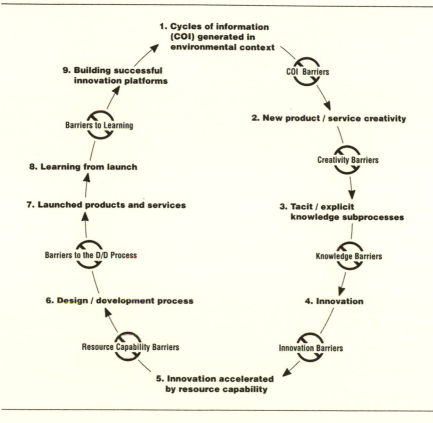

their ability to find useful and effective new ideas. In general, this view is a barrier to improving the process. The inventor/entrepreneur in the garage is one thing, but the innovation processes in major firms are too important to allow "the fuzzy front end" to be omitted from the philosophy and approach of the New Science. While this will be an unpopular view in many firms, it is important to structure and improve these processes.

Cycles of Information

The time that covers Steps 1 through 5 in the product line innovation process goes by unnoticed in most firms; it is certainly not measured. During this time, numerous cycles of information occur and opportunity abounds. As a cycle progresses, information about consumer needs bubbles up from the market, the industry, and consumers themselves. Thoughts and ideas hatched by a variety of people in the firm are seldom put forth because of the myriad barriers arising from the organization's dominant logic, dominant coalition, genetic code, and strategy shape.

These cycles of information happen on a regular basis. We estimate that the average firm experiences, but fails to notice, at least 50 cycles of information in *a month*. For some reason, most firms are deficient in the skill of opportunity recognition. Although recent advice from strategy gurus advises that firms become entrepreneurial, even revolutionary, to improve their ability to recognize opportunities, the advice does not seem to take hold.

The typical firm can become much better at noticing and taking action on cycles of information by applying the following rule of thumb: One key cycle of information containing severe "disconfirming" evidence should reach the program office at a regular frequency of between five to seven market rhythms. Disconfirming evidence is that which shocks the dominant logic and strategy shape of the company. It may be unsettling; it may be viewed as heresy; it may make the hair stand up on the back of your neck—but it is the key to innovation.

The product line innovation process contains nine steps. Each step is hindered by clearly identifiable barriers to execution. The collective prime movers in a company must spend part of their time every week identifying and removing the barriers in the first five steps. If the program office structure and a culture of executive activism are securely in place, it will be easier to activate this process than it may be to become truly entrepreneurial or revolutionary.

Step 1. Environmental Context Generates Cycles of Information

The environmental context for the innovation process is both external and internal to the firm. The external context consists of the flow of information from customers, the industry, and markets. The internal context is made up of a mixture of the dominant logic, coalition, pattern, strategy shape, and genetic code that have been established over time.

Environmental Context Barriers

The barriers to receiving information from the external context are lack of external relationships, failure to access true information as opposed to volumes of data, and ineffective communication between the firm and the outside world. Inward looking firms almost always have a difficult time with product line innovation.

The primary internal barrier is the resistance of the dominant pattern to recognize value in anything strange or unknown. The firm's executives must be willing to challenge their own dogma if they are to facilitate the innovation process.

Step 2. New Product/Service Creativity

Creativity is the skill of seeing order or a useful pattern in what most people see as chaos—and seeing it first. Although individuals can seldom increase their personal creative skills, the product line innovation process tries to offset this shortfall by gathering together all the creative ideas in the firm and putting them to use. This can happen only when barriers are removed.

Barriers to New Product/Service Creativity

There are myriad barriers to this step. Among many we have found are fear of upsetting the pattern, routine, and status quo; fear of the "shoot the messenger" phenomenon; and fear of looking stupid, childish, or naive in the eyes of the dominant coalition. Allowing the innovation process to make use of current levels of creativity alone should be justification for attacking these barriers.

Step 3. Tacit and Explicit Knowledge Subprocesses

There are two kinds of knowledge for our purposes here: tacit knowledge and explicit knowledge. Tacit knowledge is unarticulated knowledge. It includes intuition, perspectives, and beliefs held by the people in the organization. Tacit knowledge forms the mental framework that guides interpretation of external events, decision making, and behavior. Explicit knowledge, by contrast, is fully and clearly revealed. It is expressed in words that are spoken or written. Both kinds of knowledge are important if the product line innovation process is to have value. Single and double loop learning must be used to extend explicit knowledge. Tacit knowledge, because it is unspoken and value-based, usually reinforces the dominant pattern and genetic code of the firm. The innovation process must work to make tacit knowledge explicit and instill tolerance for differing perspectives and differing styles of communication, thinking, and decision making. Here the powers-of-three concept and requiring cycles of disconfirming information can help.

A creative idea must pass through several knowledge subprocesses before it emerges as tacit or explicit knowledge. The most useful subprocesses are exploratory design and proactive market development. By presenting prototypes to current customers as well as to customers in related industries, the investigators can gather immediate reactions and assess eventual intent to buy. These interactions should not be confused with traditional market research, which may be used in the design/development step of the process. These subprocesses perform rapid prototyping that can be shared with known early adopters and opinion leaders in order to proactively prepare the market for eventual acceptance. This procedure is quite similar to how seasoned venture capital firms try to assess the viability of proposed technologies.

Barriers to Knowledge Subprocesses

The biggest barriers to this step are the lack of commitment for funding and failure to grant release time for those involved with the exploratory design and market development. "Found" money from implementing the other aspects of the New Science will often provide the seed money for the prototypes and released time.

Step 4. Innovation

Innovation means bringing to the market new products and services that customers will buy. The insight, foresight, and relationships with early adopters

gained during the first three steps are *actively leveraged* in this step. The prototypes that appear to have promise are championed within the firm, and high performance teams are commissioned by the program office to incubate the opportunity.
These innovation opportunity teams should be fluid, assembled for the incubation
period alone. But they must have program office visibility. For many years, Sony
has used a system like this to support its innovative stream of new products.

Maintaining a balance between released time for special projects and completing the daily work of the firm is at the heart of execution excellence. When maintenance work becomes efficient and effective, huge costs can be eliminated. The
dollars saved can allow the release of people for work on the initiative and opportunity teams.

Barriers to Innovation

The primary barriers to innovation as defined here are, unbelievably, a disdain
for the customer and the lack of alignment and synchronicity among executive,
operating, and support processes and in their relationship to market rhythms. The
disdain for customers arises out of previous cycles of responding to customer com-
plaints and dissatisfactions, and leads to a subtle disinterest in leveraging the prototypes and proactive market actions required in Step 4. Earlier problems in the
innovation process can become magnified at this stage and diminish the drive to
put forth new ventures, which begin to be perceived as too difficult to do.

Step 5. Innovation Accelerated by Resource Capability

Resources for product line innovation are organizational processes, competencies, and funds to go outside to obtain the competencies if they do not exist in
house (e.g., using direct hires, part-time workers, and subcontractors). This may
seem like an obvious requirement, but surprisingly in many firms, it is not. People
who have a bent for creativity and innovation are hard to find, and company executives may discover that these resources are in short supply if they have not been
identified far enough ahead of the need.

Barriers to Resource Capability

Senior management often lacks an awareness of how long it takes to install a
product line innovation process with the resources that are available in house,
which negatively affects resource capability. HR can sometimes be another barrier if the resource pool is not actively assessed for the required processes, competencies, and skills.

Step 6. New Product Design/Development Process

There are hundreds of versions of processes for new product design and development. Every firm must adapt ideas from these processes to create its version. As
mentioned above, most of the steps in the process are located within the four major

phases of the initiative management process—generation, commitment, development and implementation, and realization—as discussed in Chapter 4.

Barriers to New Product Design/Development

There are two major barriers in the design/development process of most firms: poor management of actions in progress (AIP) and key executive processes that short circuit real commitment to long term continuity in developing products and services. AIPs are the top priority tasks or initiatives as determined by the figure of merit (FOM) calculation or other prioritizing mechanism. Inadequate AIP management allows people to work on pet initiatives instead of priority tasks. When these situations arise, it indicates that the firm lacks the discipline that is necessary to complete active, priority tasks before starting new ones from backlog. This kind of management discipline may be resisted as inhibiting to creativity, but the time for creativity was in the early stages of product line innovation. Now is the time for focused work in determining the appropriate product features, given the needs of customers and the price they are willing to pay.

The second major barrier in this step arises from executive processes that do not give real commitment to funding the products and services in the product line innovation pipeline. Strategic planning, forecasting, budgeting, the annual operating plan, resource allocation, and performance management may imply support, but in practice they often deny the year-to-year commitment that permits design/development resources to remain focused.

Step 7. Launched Products and Services

In this step, the products and services are launched and strive to hit their targets at world-class speed. By now, the initiative management process has taken over the implementation and realization of the new products and services. Single and double loop learnings are being gathered to arrive at the ultimate positioning and financial realization of the opportunity. At this point, both the innovation opportunity team and the initiative team are poised to learn from the results.

Step 8. Learning from Launched Products and Services

Successful learning requires a nonbureaucratic way of capturing and instilling new tacit and explicit knowledge, updating mental models, and establishing whether or not the planned innovation has become an actual innovation. The firm also needs to accumulate knowledge about what produces increases in wealth. Data warehouses and other types of information technology must be used to store these new learnings so that future innovation opportunity teams have access to the knowledge.

Step 9. Building Successful Innovation Platforms

In this last step, the owners of the firm's operating processes are introduced to cycles of information and cycles of learning so that growth in products and services can expand. They may build on a highly developed core competence (e.g., small motors at Black and Decker) or a key customer relationship (e.g., individuals of high net worth at an investment bank). These in-place skills and/or relationships serve as platforms that allow rapid growth through the development of new product families from the core competence or an increased market base of multiple customer groups derived from a single key relationship. The platforms are like launching pads of confidence and strategy that help to disperse new, winning offerings and spread them to different customer and product groups. The yield from repeated rounds of learning can range from product and service extensions to the confidence to conceive and generate bolder ideas and applications.

Feedback to the Beginning of the Product Line Innovation Process

At the end of the cycle, it is time to find ways of making improvements in the process. The goal is to get real potential innovations into design/development with speed, care, and foresight. Process improvements may include:

• Decreasing the time required by the cycles of information (Steps 1–5).

• Increasing the number of new attempts at innovation.

• Reducing cycle time, rework, and cost.

• Improving the relationship between the product line innovation process and the initiative management process.

CONCLUSION

This chapter presents a relatively straightforward process and discipline to help firms improve their ability to find, incubate, and push forward totally new products or services. The essence of the process is to install measurement and imperative into the period *before* the product design/development process begins. It requires that the tools and techniques presented throughout this book be applied: identifying barriers; measuring cycle times, rework, and costs; and using improvement in the measures to drive out barriers. The potential leverage and improvement can justify introducing and using a product line innovation process such as the one we have outlined here.

In the concluding chapter, we examine the range of improvement in sales, margins, capital avoidance, and agility that can be achieved through the broad use of the New Science of Strategy Execution.

Chapter 11

A Look Back and a Look Ahead

As we described at the beginning of this book, business leaders in the past three decades have been faced with a number of conflicting views about the very notion of strategy. In the 1970s, strategy consisted of a search for an "outlier" position as a way of securing competitive advantage. In the 1980s, strategy turned its sights on finding a position within an industry structure. Also during that decade, strategy was defined as the mechanism that could moderate between two opposing logics: the drive for the divergent, breakthrough solutions versus an emphasis on converging to central control.

In the 1990s, strategy brought us the process and culture revolutions, which were heralded as ways of developing industry foresight to discern the "white spaces" in which latent customer needs were waiting to be found. As the new century began, strategy focused on the importance of organizational culture and on the possibility of revolutionizing all aspects of the business model to gain front-runner advantage. Today, strategy also involves a search for competitive spaces in the "extended enterprise environment," building on the economics of information.

In retrospect, these varied but important approaches to strategy can be appreciated as developmental steps, leading to the platform we find ourselves on today. The New Science of Strategy Execution synthesizes key elements of many of these earlier ideas into a practical methodology that can be used by business leaders who now face challenges never thought of in previous years.

The New Science has already produced results for firms that have embraced it. These results come from improved measures in both leading indicators (drivers of success) and lagging indicators (end results). Monitoring lead measures (cycle times, rework, and cost) helps to identify process barriers. As these barriers are driven out, an improved way of working evolves and leads to more assured end results.

A TYPICAL RANGE OF PERFORMANCE IMPROVEMENT

By analyzing the results of real companies that have used all or part of the New Science, we can determine the average improvement potential as calibrated for a

$1 billion enterprise. These improvements represent *gains beyond previously planned levels*. Most of the benefits can be found by assessing the five key drivers of a firm's shareholder wealth: top line revenue growth, margin increase due to higher price points, margin increase due to cost management, capital avoidance, and agility. Table 11.1 shows a range of the average improvement we have witnessed in each driver.

Table 11.1
Improvement Potential Using the New Science of Strategy Execution

Drivers of Wealth Creation	Range of Average Improvement Beyond Planned Levels*
Top line revenue growth	4.00 – 15.0%
Margin increase due to higher price points	0.25 – 1.0%
Margin increase due to cost management	0.50 – 1.0%
Capital avoidance	10.00 – 30.0%
Agility of the firm as measured by decreased change and reduced response times	50.0%

* Based on experiences of a $1 billion enterprise.

At first glance, these improvements may seem modest. In reality, however, any improvement beyond planned levels—if additional risk is not incurred—can mean above average growth in stock prices. New Science factors that bring about the improvement in each of the measures are described below.

1. *Top Line Revenue Growth.* Extended revenue growth of 4 percent to 15 percent can be gained by implementing New Science processes. Revenue improves because the firm is able to get new products and services to market sooner *and* with higher yield or success rates (i.e., with not as much rework or relaunching) than would be possible using less focused methods. In addition, the reallocation of resources among processes facilitates initiative team success and, thus, adds to financial return.

2. *Net Margin Increase Due to Higher Price Points.* Net margin increases of 0.25 to 1.0 percentage points—measured as a percent of sales—can be traced directly to maintaining higher price points. Being first to market with products and services that are in demand allows prices to be set at premium levels and to hold steady during falling market conditions. The New Science also strengthens the firm's ability to execute better than competition, which in turn increases customers' perception of value.

3. *Net Margin Increase Due to Cost Management.* Reductions in cycle time, rework, and cost in the suite of executive, operating, and support processes also allow net margins to increase. Increased margins due to these savings can range from 0.5 to 1.0 percentage points, measured as a percent of sales.

4. *Capital Avoidance.* Applying the New Science definitions of executive productivity, efficiency, and effectiveness, and employing the discipline of the initiative management pro-

cess, greatly reduce the tendency to "throw capital" at problems. This new discipline can account for a 10 percent to 30 percent decrease in the use of capital to solve problems.

5. *Agility of the Firm*. All aspects of the New Science support the functioning of high performance teams that can change and adapt more quickly than competition. In addition, the New Science offers an improved approach to change management because it focuses on key metrics that eliminate barriers and encourages learning along the way. Firms practicing the New Science have been able to reduce the time it takes them to respond to marketplace change by an average of 50 percent.

Many of the improvements in the drivers of wealth creation are due to changes in general management. As yet, few firms have investigated the notion of making their strategy execution systems PALS with market rhythms, and many seem to consider trying to improve *executive* efficiency, productivity, and effectiveness as either unnecessary or taboo. The nagging symptoms of a myriad of problems are rooted in these processes, and *working on symptoms alone produces clutter and confusion, wastes time, and yields little*. Faults in the processes themselves must be addressed.

COMPENSATION, LEADERSHIP, AND CHANGE MANAGEMENT IN THE NEW SCIENCE

In these pages, we have not discussed at length three factors usually considered to be highly important in organizational success: executive compensation, leadership, and change management. Experience in the firms that underlie the methodology and framework of the New Science indicates that base compensation and incentives are neutral factors. They are the common denominator—mere satisfiers and not true motivators. Indeed, recent evidence suggests that granting stock options as incentives drives the wrong kinds of behavior. In addition, most employees have become quite cynical about internal efforts to reprice stock as external stock prices fall. These factors confirm the findings reported years ago by Herzberg and MacGregor: "Carrot" approaches to motivation—base and incentive compensation, options, and other perquisites—have never been shown to improve motivation or strategy execution.[1]

Executive compensation must be internally equitable and externally competitive, but world-class strategy execution requires something else. That "something else" is the processes and ways of thinking about and organizing for strategy execution that we present in this book. Most variable compensation should be based on the lead and lag measures of team and unit performance, as these measures use the "shared destiny" approach to attack the common enemy. A trigger point should be established based on the free cash flow required to support increases in the firm's value. That is, a desired level of free cash flow from operations must be set as a goal to support increases in the firm's value or stock price. If the teams surpass this trigger point, the overage should be distributed to them in a fair and equitable manner. If the trigger point is not reached, then no additional payment should be made except in the case of individuals who have gone above and beyond the call of duty *over a sus-*

tained period of time. The Central Oversight Committee (COC) should make that determination based on a nomination by peers for sustained merit.

The organization should emphasize finding people who have an intrinsic motivation to complete things and who take pride in authentic work, because these individuals and teams will be geared to the real drumbeat and economics of the business. The prime movers in a firm must also instill an unremitting insistence on action and create a shared destiny to identify and remove barriers if world-class strategy execution is to be achieved. They must use metrics and grassroots leadership to rally the organization against the common enemy of subject matter, process, structure, and culture barriers that get in the way of developing and using world-class strategy execution skills.

This is the only way a firm can become a fast, sleek wealth creator. As small wins are celebrated, execution success and confidence will build, as will the pride of being part of group of people who are doing valuable work. The pride grows not from the ephemeral slogans of a change management program but from a sense of true apprenticeship and stewardship and a craftsman's appreciation for quality work. This is what the New Science can create in firms.

The second topic we have omitted is leadership. Conventional leadership training involving understanding personal style, having a vision, and motivating people for change is fine for individual improvement. Leadership in the New Science, however, means being in the trenches to help execute the disciplines that bring about world-class strategy execution in cross-unit and cross-process teams. Leadership from this perspective cannot be learned in a classroom; it is voluntary and is best learned in an apprentice role.

Leaders of the New Science are willing to work alongside their troops. They have the courage to accept responsibility if things go wrong. In this way, both the leaders and their organizations learn. Leaders of the New Science prioritize, lead the charge, and set an example of discipline and fairness. They can say no without weakening motivation. The best leadership training for achieving the results we describe here is through active apprenticeships. Involving people in the ongoing processes, tools, and methods of the New Science allows them to move quickly from novice to master, if there are masters who can lead and show the way.

Our omission of an in-depth discussion of change management was deliberate. In practice, it appears that popular approaches, while tantalizing, are not adequate for instilling real change. These efforts involve creating what is sometimes called a "burning platform"—an uncomfortable situation that makes people prefer an uncertain future over the status quo. But changes that are motivated in this way never really stick, if they happen at all. One of the major problems with these practices is that people are not given daily and weekly tools and encouragement with a real, common enemy to focus on. In addition, these conventional methods are almost always involved with classic situations of initiative overload (sometimes as a test of the ability to handle massive change)—the very anathema of the New Science. The approach we present here is much simpler:

- Rally people around the common enemy—subject matter, process, structure, and culture barriers that cause cycle times, rework, and cost to be too high in all business processes.

- Set the right metrics so that individuals and teams can drive the barriers out by improving appropriate leading (driver) and lagging (end result) measures.

- Create cockpit charts to measure improvement weekly and report monthly.

- Celebrate small wins and suitably praise and reward true high performers, while helping everyone to improve through cycles of learning and confidence.

- As the platform of confidence and success grows, take on bigger, broader, and bolder initiatives.

A LOOK TO THE FUTURE

As the business environment changes, new challenges will arise and new ideas will come forth to meet them. As our strategy knowledge grows and as more firms have experience with the New Science, we will be able to refine our understanding of the causes and effects of change. Already it seems clear that further work in the areas of grassroots leadership and product line innovation would help to improve the New Science principles.

There is also a huge opportunity in improving our understanding of the forces of integrity and magnanimity as they are applied in the seven stages of growth and continuous improvement. The pressure for quarterly earnings is insidious, but can be resisted if the leadership and prime movers of a firm hold to their belief that current strategies are best for the long term. By holding the line in difficult times, executives can demonstrate the power of taking the right action at the right time, given the economic climate they face. The brief survey suggested in Chapter 6 may seem threatening to management teams until they begin to see the benefits of honest and direct feedback. Once the notions of integrity and magnanimity begin to inform security analysts' decisions, they will have a better way to assess the fundamental strategic and operating health of a company.

Many aspects of the New Science can provide important insights and additions to the growing field of executive education. The New Science can totally reshape the timing of such training, the function of "action and results" learning assignments, and the role of the initiative management process in moving promising initiatives through the system. Executive education can help create an "execution culture" as well.

The next vista for research is to gather more data on the impact of the New Science on the leading and lagging indicators of performance and to collect the success stories to stimulate further learning.

NOTE

1. Frederick Herzberg, Bernard Mausner, and Barbara Bloch Snyderman, *The Motivation to Work*, 2nd ed. (New York: John Wiley, 1959); Douglas MacGregor, *The Human Side of Enterprise* (New York: McGraw Hill, 1960).

APPENDIXES

Appendix 1

Customer Research Approach to Estimating Buying Cycles and Market Rhythms

To the reader: This questionnaire has been designed to assist you in estimating your current buying cycles and market rhythms as discussed in Chapters 2 and 3 of this book. If yours is a business-to-business firm, ask a senior executive from a top customer firm in each of your product or service categories to complete the form and return it to you. If you are a retail firm selling directly to consumers, interview a sample of your best customers to gather information for the calculation.

To score: Average the frequencies on questions 2–3 on all questionnaires to determine the buying cycle. Average the frequencies on questions 4–9 on all questionnaires to find the market rhythm and compare it to the buying cycle. The frequencies will usually be four to five times faster than the buying cycle. It is the market rhythm that sets the standard for executive, operating, and support process alignment and synchronization.

CUSTOMER SATISFACTION STUDY

Please help us to improve our customer service. Review the following questions and respond based on the situation at the present time. We thank you for your time and your input.

1. List the five most important *and* most frequent items you purchased from our company in the last calendar or fiscal year.

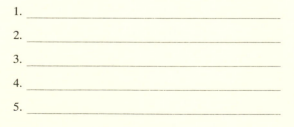

   1. _____

   2. _____

   3. _____

   4. _____

   5. _____

2. How often do you purchase or pay a recurring bill for each item?

    1. _____

    2. _____

    3. _____

    4. _____

    5. _____

3a. Over the past year, how often were you *dissatisfied with the each purchased item?*
How great was your dissatisfaction? (5 = highly dissatisfied 1 = mildly dissatisfied)
What was the reason for your dissatisfaction?

Frequency	*Strength*	*Reason*
1.		
2.		
3.		
4.		
5.		

3b. Over the last year, how often were you *dissatisfied each time you purchased it on a recurring basis?*

Frequency	*Strength*	*Reason*
1.		
2.		
3.		
4.		
5.		

3c. Over the last year, how often were you *dissatisfied with the payment/billing cycle for the item?*

Frequency	*Strength*	*Reason*
1.		
2.		
3.		
4.		
5.		

4. Over the past year, how often did a competing vendor/retailer for each of the purchased items try to convince you directly to switch vendors?

How strongly did you consider switching? (Strong consideration = 5, No consideration = 1)

Item	Frequency	Strength
1.		
2.		
3.		
4.		
5.		

5. Over the last year, how often did you receive a piece of marketing material from a competing vendor/retailer for each of the purchased items?

How strongly did you consider switching based on the marketing material alone? (Strong consideration = 5, No consideration = 1)

Item	Frequency	Strength
1.		
2.		
3.		
4.		
5.		

6. How often did you use the Internet last year?

_____

During that year, how often did you visit the website of a competing vendor/retailer for each item?

_____

7. Over the last year, how often did you think about finding a better way to obtain and use each of the purchased items?

1. _____

2. _____

3. _____

4. _____

5. _____

8. Over the past year, how often did you think about finding a less expensive way of obtaining and using each of the purchased items?

    1. _____

    2. _____

    3. _____

    4. _____

    5. _____

9. Over the past year, how often did you feel you were being taken advantage of by continuing to purchase each of the items from your current vendor/retailer?

    1. _____

    2. _____

    3. _____

    4. _____

    5. _____

10. What would make you switch to a competitor's product for each item?

    1. _____

    2. _____

    3. _____

    4. _____

    5. _____

11. What would have to happen to make you stop purchasing and using each item altogether?

    1. _____

    2. _____

    3. _____

    4. _____

    5. _____

Appendix 2

Managing Ripple Effects by Assessing the Eleven Modules of Business Performance

The eleven modules shown below describe the forces for change in a firm. Identifying these forces and their relative order facilitates predicting the timing of major change as discussed in Chapter 8. The laws of competitive dynamics and basic human nature determine the timing of change as the organization works to ensure that its financial objectives are reached. Change in one module (a mega-burst) can cause change in other modules (micro-bursts). This appendix provides a list of questions that can be used to assess the status of each module at a given time. The individual module assessments can be used as a baseline for comparison, as an early warning of unexpected change, or as a way of managing planned change. The cumulative assessment across all modules provides a picture of the positive and negative aspects of the firm's current status.

1. THE STADIUM IN WHICH THE FIRM COMPETES

The stadium in which a firm competes represents forces that exist outside the firm's boundaries and over which the firm has the least control. The stadium includes *general influences*, such as political, economic, social, and cultural effects, and *industry specific influences* such technology, competition, and customers.

A. Current industry trajectory. Select one of more of the following descriptors as it applies to your industry.

- Runaway growth

- Free fall to disaster

- Mushroom, and then die

- Phoenix rising from the ashes

- Solid growth

- In the doldrums, but still attractive

- Slow death

- Under attack from a well-financed/strong competitor

- Under attack from a subsidized individual competitor

- Under attack from a predatory competitor

- Regulated industry setting

- Recently deregulated setting

- Subsidized industry setting

B. Sales pattern/flow over time

- Even sales spread over time

- Seasonal sales

- Cyclical sales

- Up and down sales, but unpredictable

- "Lumpy" sales—one big ticket sale occurring sporadically

C. Nature of competitive rivalry

- Benign

- Polite, but ever present

- Intense

- Hostile

- Predatory—trying to drive you out of business

2. STRATEGIC FINANCIAL PARADIGM

Your strategic financial paradigm (SFP) is the persistent financial sense of urgency that exists in and around the top management team. Your SFP is determined partly by the stadium and partly by the solutions to issues in the other nine modules.

A. Burn rate of cash

High   Medium   Low

B. Added value/sales ratio (actual return – required return/sales)

High   Medium   Low

C. Tier size in terms of asset/fixed cost base

High   Medium   Low

3. ROLES OF CEO AND TOP MANAGEMENT TEAM

Members of the top management team (TMT) must assume three crucial roles at all times—Architect, Master Builder and Visionary. The Architect is the person who designs the organization's *form*, including structure, control systems, and information processes. The Master Builder is the person who blends together processes and people to achieve results. The Visionary is the person with foresight and creativity who intuitively understands the trends underlying changes in customers' buying patterns and projects the impact of those shifts. The exact nature of these roles will be determined directly by the stadium and strategic financial paradigm and indirectly by the other modules of organizational activity. Rarely will one person fill all three roles. Instead, team members with complementary styles take on the roles.

Is there sufficient and appropriate allocation of effort, energy, and inspiration among members of the TMT to fulfill these roles?

A: Architect

Yes   No   Somewhat

B: Master Builder

Yes   No   Somewhat

C. Visionary

Yes   No   Somewhat

4. CUSTOMER INTIMACY, LOYALTY, AND PROFITABILITY PROFILE

This profile is the firm's honest philosophy about the importance of providing superior value, satisfaction, and quality to ensure customer loyalty. This philosophy emerges most directly from the conditions in the first three modules; the truth sometimes surprises a TMT as problems arise in those modules.

A. Customer value (Benefits − Price = + from the customer's perspective)

1. Is this philosophy of customer loyalty a way of life in the TMT?

        Yes   No   Somewhat

2. Is this philosophy of customer loyalty a way of life in the rest of the firm?

        Yes   No   Somewhat

B: Customer satisfaction (actual delivery/expected delivery > 1 from the customer's perspective)

1. Is this philosophy of customer loyalty a way of life in the TMT?

        Yes   No   Somewhat

2. Is this philosophy of customer loyalty a way of life in the rest of the firm?

        Yes   No   Somewhat

C. Quality = Six Sigma achievement around customer value + customer satisfaction

1. Is this philosophy of customer loyalty a way of life in the TMT?

        Yes   No   Somewhat

2. Is this philosophy of customer loyalty a way of life in the rest of the firm?

        Yes   No   Somewhat

5. COMMUNICATING AND WINNING THROUGH STRATEGIC MARKETING

This module assesses whether or not there is a program that provides a total communication package to each distinct group of customers and whether a true relationship and consultative selling culture exists to keep targeted customer groups loyal and profitable.

A. "3rd decimal point" marketing

Is there a total communications strategy for each major homogeneous customer group?

        Yes   No

B. Involvement of marketing with the strategic foundation and value delivery system

Do marketing communications reflect the true competencies and value delivery system of the firm?

        Yes   No

C. Interfaces of A. and B. on consultative selling

Does a true culture of consultative selling relationships exist with key customers?

        Yes   No

6. STRATEGY IN FIVES

With the cumulative energy and mindset of the TMT focused on the first five modules, the team can then turn to organizing strategic thinking and decision making around five interlocked aspects of strategy formulation. These categories offer an effective way to communicate the strategic intent and direction of your firm to the rest of the organization.

A. Grand strategy—Purpose, Vision, Mission

1. Can the TMT articulate the purpose, vision, and mission, and do these strategies serve as a unique catalyst and focus for thought leadership and strategic action?

        Yes   No   Somewhat

2. Can the rest of the firm articulate the purpose, vision, and mission and do these strategies serve as a unique catalyst for thought leadership and strategic action?

        Yes   No   Somewhat

B. Mission-level strategy—Method of competition, desired leadership position, scale/critical mass, scope, cost structure and position, philosophy about required rate of return, need and capacity for sharing among business units, functions, departments

1. Can the TMT articulate these aspects of strategy and do these aspects serve as a unique catalyst and focus for thought leadership and strategic action?

        Yes   No   Somewhat

2. Can the rest of the firm articulate these aspects of strategy and do these aspects serve as a unique catalyst for thought leadership and strategic action?

   Yes   No   Somewhat

C. Action strategy—Goals, objectives, initiatives, programs, projects

1. Can the TMT articulate these elements of action and do these elements serve as a unique catalyst and focus for thought leadership and strategic action?

   Yes   No   Somewhat

2. Can the rest of the firm articulate these elements of action and do these elements serve as a unique catalyst for thought leadership and strategic action?

   Yes   No   Somewhat

D. Reengineering (incremental or revolutionary change in structure and/or process)

1. Can the TMT articulate the reengineering focus and does that focus serve as a unique catalyst and focus for thought leadership and strategic action?

   Yes   No   Somewhat

2. Can the rest of the firm articulate the reengineering focus and does that focus serve as a unique catalyst for thought leadership and strategic action?

   Yes   No   Somewhat

E. Key emerging topics (technology, accounting standard changes, regulatory challenges, etc.)

1. Can the TMT articulate key emerging topics and do these topics serve as a unique catalyst and focus for thought leadership and strategic action?

   Yes   No   Somewhat

2. Can the rest of the firm articulate key emerging topics and do these topics serve as a unique catalyst for thought leadership and strategic action?

   Yes   No   Somewhat

7. ORGANIZATIONAL EFFECTIVENESS SYSTEM

This module houses a firm's total capabilities to deliver superior customer value, satisfaction, and quality and to sustain owner wealth. This system includes solutions to structure, processes, climate and culture, and recognition, reward, and people. The firm's "genetic code" is located in this module, and deep barriers can reside here.

A. Structure

1. Is the current structure useful?

   Yes   No   Somewhat

2. Are the parts of the current structure aligned with one another?

   Yes   No   Somewhat

3. Which structures are not useful?

4. Which parts are not aligned?

5. What barriers prevent the parts of the structure from being useful and aligned?

B. People

1. Is the current organization of people useful?

   Yes   No   Somewhat

2. Are the efforts of people aligned with one another?

   Yes   No   Somewhat

3. Which parts of the organization are not useful?

4. Which efforts are not aligned?

5. What barriers prevent the entire organization from being useful and aligned?

C. Recognition and reward

1. Are the current policies and practices of recognition and reward useful?

   Yes   No   Somewhat

2. Are the current policies and practices aligned with one another?

   Yes   No   Somewhat

3. Which policies or procedures are not useful?

4. Which policies or procedures are not aligned?

5. What barriers prevent policies and procedures from being useful and aligned?

D. Processes

1. Are the current processes useful?

        Yes   No   Somewhat

2. Are the current processes aligned with one another?

        Yes   No   Somewhat

3. Which processes are not useful?

4. Which processes are not aligned?

5. What barriers prevent processes from being useful and aligned?

E. Culture

1. Is the current culture useful?

        Yes   No   Somewhat

2. Are all elements of the culture aligned with one another?

        Yes   No   Somewhat

3. Which elements of the culture are not useful?

4. Which elements of the culture are not aligned?

5. What barriers prevent elements of the culture from being useful and aligned?

8. DRIVERS OF SUSTAINABLE COMPETITIVE ADVANTAGE

This module uses an open systems model to depict the areas that reveal when and where your firm is "driving" against direct and indirect competitors and where resource leverage may exist. These drivers represent the root causes for your firm's current performance level.

1. Relative to the best competitor with which the firm competes, check below the drivers that help to provide superior thought leadership and control customer or product platform opportunities and/or current market power position.

2. Relative to the best competitor, check the drivers below that detract from providing superior thought leadership and control of customer or product platform opportunities and/or current market power position.

- Marketing drivers   Help ___   Detract ___
- New product process drivers   Help ___   Detract ___
- R&D drivers   Help ___   Detract ___
- Operating process drivers   Help ___   Detract ___
- People drivers   Help ___   Detract ___
- Structure drivers   Help ___   Detract ___
- Compensation drivers   Help ___   Detract ___
- Culture drivers   Help ___   Detract ___
- Information technology drivers   Help ___   Detract ___
- Total quality (Six Sigma) drivers Help ___   Detract ___
- Customer service drivers   Help ___   Detract ___
- Command of input resources drivers Help ___   Detract ___
- Alliance/joint venture drivers   Help ___   Detract ___
- Total cycle time drivers   Help ___   Detract ___

9. MAXIMIZATION OF SHAREHOLDER/OWNER WEALTH GAME BOARD

All of the previous modules are evaluated in this module for their contribution to the firm's ability to earn more than its required rate of return. Firms in this enviable position are wealth creators and enjoy many economic benefits.

1. List the value drivers that have been and are expected to continue improving.

2. List the value drivers that have been and are expected to continue faltering.

3. Is there a useful blend of entrepreneurial spirit and the control of risk and uncertainty?

Compare your reality with the positive direction shown for each factor below.

Direction Required for Wealth Creation

1. Sales growth rate   ↑

2. Operating profit margin   ↑

3. Income tax rate   ↓

4. Incremental working capital investment   ↓

5. Incremental fixed capital investment   ↓

6. Required ROR on equity (based on firm's risk class) ↓

7. Sustainability of favorable directions in 1-6   ↑

10. ENTREPRENEURIAL STRATEGY DEVELOPMENT PROCESS

This process is a comprehensive system that unites strategic thinking, strategic planning, and strategic decision making to support and synthesize all of the decisions, energy, and focus from the previous modules. The process also lays a foundation that ensures that all the requirements necessary for successfully competing in the future are made available to the TMT and other opinion leaders and process champions in a timely, user friendly, and value added manner.

A. System format, calendar, specific deliverables

1. Does a useful plan exist for these factors that is consistent with modules 1–9 and 11?

    Yes   No   Somewhat

2. Which plans are useful and value added?

3. Which plans are not useful and add no value?

B. Decision/approval processes

1. Does a useful procedure exist for these processes that is consistent with modules 1–9 and 11?

    Yes   No   Somewhat

2. Which procedures are useful and value added?

3. Which procedures are not useful and add no value?

C. Inter-accountabilities

1. Does a useful procedure exist for this factor that is consistent with modules 1–9 and 11?

    Yes   No   Somewhat

2. Which procedures are useful and value added?

3. Which procedures are not useful and add no value?

D. Resource allocation process

1. Does a useful procedure exist for this process that is consistent with modules 1–9 and 11?

    Yes   No   Somewhat

2. Which procedures are useful and value added?

3. Which procedures are not useful and add no value?

E. Budgeting process and system

1. Does a useful procedure exist for this system that is consistent with modules 1–9 and 11?

> Yes   No   Somewhat

2. Which procedures are useful and value added?

3. Which procedures are not useful and add no value?

F. Use of Intranet/Internet for enablement

1. Does a useful procedure exist for this factor that is consistent with modules 1–9 and 11?

> Yes   No   Somewhat

2. Which procedures are useful and value added?

3. Which procedures are not useful and add no value?

G. Relationships/contracts with operations

1. Does a useful procedure exist for these factors that is consistent with modules 1–9 and 11?

> Yes   No   Somewhat

2. Which procedures are useful and value added?

3. Which procedures are not useful and add no value?

11. HIGH PERFORMANCE TEAM CHALKBOARD

This last module allows your company to come together as a Team of High Performance Teams with focus, clarity, direction, energy, and leadership. It is the people catalyst for getting things done today and for starting new opportunity/initiative cycles for future performance.

A. Which functions/processes/geographic areas have power/visibility?

1. Do you have a way of ensuring team power and visibility consistent with the needs of modules 1–10?

2. Which methods are useful?

3. Which methods are not useful?

B. Correct number of teams

1. Do you have a way of creating the optimal number of teams required by modules 1–10?

2. Which methods are useful?

3. Which methods are not useful?

C. Team make-up

1. Do you have a way of creating teams with the make up required by modules 1–10?

2. Which methods are useful?

3. Which methods are not useful?

D. Readiness to be a team

1. Do you have a way of ensuring team readiness as required by modules 1–10?

2. Which methods are useful?

3. Which methods are not useful?

E. Ways to provide interconnectedness among teams

1. Do you have a way of interconnecting teams as required by modules 1–10?

2. Which methods are useful?

3. Which methods are not useful?

F. Ways to measure team performance

1. Do you have a useful way of measuring team performance in modules 1–10?

2. Which methods are useful?

3. Which methods are not useful?

Appendix 3

Using the Eleven Modules of Business Performance for Dynamic Strategic Planning and Execution: A Case Study

This case study describes the actual results of strategic planning exercises conducted by the ABC company (a pseudonym). This case study illustrates the process described in Chapter 8 and Appendix 2.

In 1995, an "advance change team," appointed by ABC's chairman, used the eleven modules of business performance to create a blueprint for moving forward to 2000. At the time of the analysis, ABC had been part of a large defense technology company for 22 years. The company was a leader in managing worldwide, diverse workforces and providing quality people to locations all over the world, at critical times and at the best value. These competencies specialized in chaotic world environments and were applied to Base Operations/Maintenance, Aircraft Overhaul/Modification, Contractor Logistics Support, and Systems Integration. Thus, ABC's core competencies centered on project and program management.

The strategic intent of the ABC team was to transform the company from a primarily government vendor serving selected growth markets to a broad-based vendor serving diverse global markets including commercial entities. The accompanying figure provides a "backcast." That is, it offers a backward look at both the analysis made in 1995 (time period T-0) with the future state in the year 2000 (time period T-5), as proposed by the ABC team. At this writing, it is 2003, and we can examine the team's projections with 20-20 hindsight. In retrospect, they seem to have been prescient in many areas, but missed a few key ripple effects and aspects of planned change management.

The ABC team's work developed from an analysis of Core Competencies, Industry Drivers, White Space Opportunities and Strategic Intent. This process was based on the ideas of Gary Hamel that were documented in *Competing for the Future*, a book he wrote with C. K. Prahalad. During the time the author was part of the Management Consulting Services unit of EDS, Hamel was consulting there

ABC's Assessment at T – 0 and Projections for T – 5

T – 0 = 1995 The situation when analysis was performed	**T – 5 = 2000** Projection of the probable future state
CORE COMPETENCIES T – 0 • *Managing a diverse, worldwide workforce.* (In 42-50 states, Central America, Europe, and Asia) • *Placing the right people in the right place at the right time for the right price.* (More than 3,500 highly skilled technicians tasked with providing sophisticated support services for the U.S. government, states, and foreign entities.) **Contracting Logistical Support** • *Base operations and management.* (Manage and operate infrastructures equal to the size of a small city.) • *Aircraft overhaul and modification.* (Fixed wing and rotor of any size) • *Managing in chaotic environments.* (Desert Storm, Somalia, Haiti, Rwanda, and Bosnia)	**CORE COMPETENCIES T – 5** • *Managing a diverse, worldwide workforce.* (For government and commercial applications.) • *Placing the right people in the right place at the right time for the right price.* (With emphasis on commercialization, ABC will become more diverse in its ability to provide skilled and unskilled labor for its customers.) **Contracting Logistical Support** • *Base operations and management.* (Expect a continuation in government, with transformation into commercial applications.) • *Aircraft overhaul and modification.* (By gaining expertise in more demanding environments, ABC will be able to offer quality services at lower prices than commercial customers are used to paying.) • *Managing in chaotic environments.* (Expect continued support to government customers. As government transforms to more commercial operations, ABC will be there supporting commercial corporations with management and service capabilities tailored to fit the mission.)
INDUSTRY DRIVERS T – 0 • *Declining Defense Industry.* (America is collecting on the peace dividend by cutting back on military size and its supporting infrastructure weapons systems.) • *Base Realignment and Closures (BRAC).* (Base closings will not end until turn of the century. Most of the facilities being closed had outlived their purpose and should have been closed long ago.) • *Changing Geopolitical Uncertainty/Instability.* (The former Soviet Union, Eastern Block Nations, China, Korea, Central and South America, Cuba, Haiti, Rwanda, Angola—The world is constantly changing.) • *Rapid Downsizing of Defense Industries.* (Mergers, acquisitions, hostile takeovers, and bankruptcy are becoming common in the defense industry.) • *Vague National Strategic Objectives.* (With the Berlin Wall gone and the Soviet threat diminished, the U.S. has no real military strategic objectives. There is no one bad guy anymore, only many smaller ones.) • *Base Closure and Realignment Trauma.* (Local communities are being devastated by the loss of jobs and revenue to the local community.) • *Service Career Path Uncertainty.* (With all the turmoil in the government, quality people are hesitant to commit to a career in the defense industry.) • *Gerrymandering of missions and weapons procurement.*	**INDUSTRY DRIVERS T – 5** • *Best Value Service Providers.* (ABC is accustomed to playing in this environment and should adapt quickly to the requirements of the commercial world.) • *Aggressive Outsourcing, Commercialization and Standardization of Service Requirements.* (Strategic alliances, teaming, partnerships, subcontracts, and joint ventures will be required to meet the commercial challenges.) • *Shared Financial Risk Between Government and Subcontractors.* (As federal budgets get smaller, the government is expecting industry to invest more capital dollars. Industry should expect higher margins based on the risk associated with this arrangement.) • *Leaner, More Efficient Defense Industry.* (Mergers, acquisitions, hostile takeovers, and strategic alliances will still be taking place in the 21st century.) • *Ongoing Base Realignment and Closures (BRAC).* • *Changing Geopolitical Uncertainty/Instability.* (This may be never ending based on human nature.) • *Downsizing of Defense Industries.* • *Vague National Military Strategic Objectives.* • *Economies of Scale.* • *Expanding Derivative Markets, i.e., outside of U.S. Government.* (By transferring knowledge and expertise to commercial applications, ABC's transformation process will be smoother than competitors going in the same direction.)

T – 0 = 1995 The situation when analysis was performed	T – 5 = 2000 Projection of the probable future state
WHITE SPACE OPPORTUNITIES T – 0 • *Develop Derivative Commercial Markets.* (Many of the skills manifested in performing government contracts are transportable to commercial applications.) • *Commercial Cargo and Transportation Services.* • *Fleet Maintenance.* • *State and Local Government Operations.* • *Privatization of Foreign Government Operations.* • *Global Positioning Systems (GPS).* • *Supporting UN Peace Initiatives.*	**WHITE SPACE OPPORTUNITIES T – 5** • *Global Derivative (non-federal) Services.* • *Global Air Traffic Control Services.* • *Global Airport Management Services.* • *Motor Pool Operations Services for State/Local Governments.* • *Road Maintenance Services for State/Local Government.* • *Rent-A-Cop Private Security Services.* • *Border Surveillance Services.* • *Hazardous Material Management Services.* • *Post Office Operations Services.*
STRATEGIC INTENT T – 0 To be the premier, worldwide provider of operations, maintenance, logistics, and systems integration services *in selected growth markets*, both government and commercial.	**STRATEGIC INTENT T – 5** To be the premier, worldwide provider of operations, maintenance, logistics, and systems integration services *in selected, diverse global growth markets*, both government and commercial.

to apply these ideas, and the author was able to observe this laboratory first-hand, helping several EDS business units apply the framework. By itself, the framework is useful as a strategic tool, but it does not include any information on strategy execution. Marrying the Hamel framework with the disciplines of the New Science—the initiative management process (Chapter 4), making executive processes PALS with market rhythms (Chapter 5), laying out a growth and innovation journey (Chapter 6), calibrating key initiative thrusts with competitive environment attractiveness (Chapter 7), and the analysis using the eleven modules (Chapter 8)—allowed the team to produce the single most useful analysis of the business ABC had ever seen. The completed assessment using the questions contained in Appendix 2 follows.

ABC'S ASSESSMENT BASED ON
THE ELEVEN MODULES OF BUSINESS PERFORMANCE

1. The Stadium in Which the Firm Competes

The stadium includes general influences, such as political, economic, social, and cultural effects, and industry specific influences, such as technology, competition, and customers.

A. Industry trajectory T-0: In the doldrums, but still attractive • Base realignment and closures (BRAC).	**A. Industry trajectory T-5:** Solid growth • Expanded opportunities as a result of government and commercial outsourcing. • Partnerships with local governments.
B. Sales pattern/flow over time T-0: "Lumpy" sales—one big ticket sale occurring sporadically.	**B. Sales pattern/flow over time T-5:** "Lumpy" sales—one big ticket sale occurring sporadically. • Predominantly sales of large projects.
C. Nature of competitive rivalry T-0: Intense • Limited number of very strong and well-finaced competitors. • No single dominant player in arena.	**C. Nature of competitive revalry T-5:** Intense • Limited number of very strong and well-financed competitors. • No single dominant player in arena. • Number of competitors will increase because of entry into derivative markets. • Possible mergers.

2. Strategic Financial Paradigm

The strategic financial paradigm (SFP) is the persistent financial sense of urgency that exists in and around the top management team.

A. Burn rate of cash T-0: High • Contractors must finance cash flow on each project for a miminum of 30 days. On larger programs, millions of dollars must be invested for short periods of time.	**A. Burn rate of cash T-5:** High • No change.
B. Added value/sales ratio (Actual return – Required return/Sales) T-0: Medium • Strictly a result of government and industry competition.	**B. Added value/sales ratio (Actual return – Required return/Sales) T-5:** Medium • No change.
C. Tier size in terms of asset/fixed cost base T-0: Medium • Minimal assets and fixed costs are small. This condition is necessary in the service industry to remain competitive. 5% is the norm.	**C. Tier size in terms of asset/fixed cost base T-5:** Medium • No change.

3. Roles of CEO and Top Management Team

Members of the top management team (TMT) must assume three crucial roles at all times: Architect, who designs the organization's form; Master Builder, who blends together processes and people to achieve results; and Visionary, who intuitively understands the trends underlying changes in customers' buying patterns. Is there sufficient and appropriate allocation of effort, energy, and inspiration among members of the TMT to fulfill these roles?

A. Architect T-0: Somewhat • Forming joint ventures and spin-off to pursue international business.	**A. Architect T-5:** Yes • Required to aggressively identify and pursue white space opportunities to remain viable business.
B. Master Builder T-0: Yes • Focus of the management team within the boundaries of current industry paradigms. Conservative approach to long-term planning. Risk averse.	**B. Master Builder T-5:** Yes • Must develop world-class strategy execution skills to turn plans into reality.
C. Visionary T-0: Somewhat • Development of special project initiative team to search for white space opportunities (Getting Broader and Bolder).	**C. Visionary T-5:** Yes • Must have the courage to continuously explore white space opportunities (Getting Bolder) in the future and use the Initiative Management Process.

4. Customer Intimacy, Loyalty, and Profitability Profile

This profile is the firm's honest philosophy about the importance of providing superior value, satisfaction, and quality to ensure customer loyalty.

A. Customer value (Benefits – Price = + from the customer's perspective) T-0	**A. Customer value (Benefits – Price = + from the customer's perspective) T-5**
1. *Is this philosophy of customer loyalty a way of life in the TMT?* Yes • Best value is judged by customer as the highest quality at lowest price. TMT focuses on these factors. Actual customer loyalty is constrained due to government imposed competitive nature of the procurement process. 2. *Is this philosophy of customer loyalty a way of life in the rest of the firm?* Yes. • Management-exempt field leaders are brought in periodically to coordinate and communicate value and satisfaction objectives.	1. *Is this philosophy of customer loyalty a way of life in the TMT?* Yes • Best value will be judged by customer as the highest quality at the lowest price. TMT will continue to focus on these factors. 2. *Is this philosophy of customer loyalty a way of life in the rest of the firm?* Yes. • Migration to commercial derivative market will require individual/team compensation to be aligned with a greater variety of customer valued business objectives.
B: Customer satisfaction (Actual delivery/ expected delivery > 1 from the customer's perspective) T-0	**B: Customer satisfaction (Actual delivery/ expected delivery > 1 from the customer's perspective) T-5**
1. *Is this philosophy of customer loyalty a way of life in the TMT?* Yes • Highly developed focus on customer satisfaction based on strict monitoring of contract compliance. Frequent auditing of activities through acceptable quality levels (AQL), for example, AQL specifies grass will be kept mowed to a certain height limit. 2. *Is this philosophy of customer loyalty a way of life in the rest of the firm?* Yes • Close coordination with TMT criteria.	1. *Is this philosophy of customer loyalty a way of life in the TMT?* Yes • Government criteria for customer satisfaction is currently well defined; however, as migration to commercial derivative markets occurs, customer surveys using the American Customer Satisfaction Index (ASCI) will be performed and documented before and after the project is completed. The satisfaction index will be used to partially compensate the individual/team performing the work. 2. *Is this philosophy of customer loyalty a way of life in the rest of the firm?* Yes • Close coordination will be required between the customer and ABC employees to achieve overall customer satisfaction objectives.

C. Quality = Six Sigma achievement around customer value + customer satisfaction T-0	C. Quality = Six Sigma achievement around customer value + customer satisfaction T-5
1. *Is this philosophy of customer loyalty a way of life in the TMT?* Yes • As measured by strict criteria for quality levels and availability based on a variety of factors balanced with agreed upon cost criteria, that is, operational readiness.	1. *Is this philosophy of customer loyalty a way of life in the TMT?* Yes • Quality and customer loyalty will require the TMT to focus on achieving diverse value and satisfaction goals for an expanding customer base.

5. Communicating and Winning Through Strategic Marketing

This module assesses whether or not there is a program that provides a total communication package to each distinct group of customers and whether a true relationship and consultative selling culture exists to keep targeted customer groups loyal and profitable.

A. "3rd decimal point" marketing (A total communications strategy for each major homogeneous customer group) T-0: Yes	A. "3rd decimal point" marketing (A total communications strategy for each major homogeneous customer group) T-5: Yes, but caution
• Marketing specialists focus on specific customer entities down to individual command and user. • Field program directors act as marketers for their specific areas.	• Effective marketing will require a broader, more detailed focus on the specific needs of a variety of customers with nongovernment service requirements and expectations. Current government marketing specialists will be supplemented with specialists in commercial service marketing. Industry specialization and alignment will be required to meet customer demands. • Field program directors will take on a more consultative role in addressing their specific customer's service needs.
B. Involvement of marketing with the strategic foundation and value delivery system T-0: Yes	B. Involvement of marketing with the strategic foundation and value delivery system T-5: Yes, with caution
• Highly tailored approach to specific market areas. • Close, face-to-face working relationship with the customer on a daily basis; requirements and value-added services are continually identified and put into the IMP.	• The current, highly tailored approach to specific market areas will continue, but the number of market areas will expand greatly. The role of the marketing function will become more important in identifying and developing these new market opportunities for the future through the IMP. • To achieve penetration and success in new arenas will require marketing to successfully communicate the unique competencies of ABC. Marketing must be able to translate ABC's

	traditional competencies and successes in the government world to clear value-added services in the commercial world. ABC strengths must be prioritized to match customers' value priorities.
C. Interfaces of A. and B. on consultative selling T-0: Yes	**C. Interfaces of A. and B. on consultative selling T-5:** Yes, with caution • Consultative marketing and selling will be an absolute must if ABC is to capture markets outside of the federal government market. Consultative selling will be required to learn the new market opportunities, develop services and strategies to address the opportunities, and promote the solutions to new customers.

6. Strategy in Fives

These categories offer an effective way to communicate the strategic intent and direction of the firm to the rest of the organization.

A. Grand strategy (Purpose, vision, mission) T-0	A. Grand strategy (Purpose, vision, mission) T-5
1. *Do these strategies serve as a unique catalyst and focus for thought leadership and strategic action?* Yes 2. *Can the rest of the firm articulate the purpose, vision, and mission?* No. • Understanding of grand strategy is limited to corporate HQ and select field positions; most field personnel do not have a clear understanding beyond their individual unit focus.	1. *Do these strategies serve as a unique catalyst and focus for thought leadership and strategic action?* Yes, but extreme caution • Five years hence, ABC's TMT will have to establish a strong grand strategy to be successful in capturing new markets. Pursuing these new markets will be a significant business and cultural change for ABC. The ability to communicate the grand strategy throughout the firm will be crucial to its execution. 2. *Can the rest of the firm articulate the purpose, vision, and mission?* Yes, but extreme caution. • The rest of the firm must have a clear understanding of the grand strategy. Many of those who have worked in the government markets for years will have to learn, understand, and adapt. This is critical for ABC, since these are the people who form the core competence of the company. Transferring these competencies to commercial markets requires alignment to the purpose, vision, and mission from top to bottom.
B. Mission-level strategy (Method of competition, desired leadeship position, scale/critical mass, scope, cost structure and position, philosophy about required rate of return, nee, and capacity for sharing among business units, functions, departments) T-0 1. *Can the TMT articulate these aspects of strategy?* Yes	**B. Mission-level strategy (Method of competition, desired leadership position, scale/critical mass, scope, cost structure and position, philosophy about required rate of return, need, and capacity for sharing among business units, functions, departments) T-5** 1. *Can the TMT articulate these aspects of strategy?* Yes, but extreme caution

- Much of this focus is required due the structured arena in which ABC competes.
2. *Do these aspects serve as a unique catalyst for thought leadership and strategic action?* Somewhat
   - Limited understanding based on level within the organization.
   - Focus is on requirements that drive the individual operating units.

- Execution of the grand strategy is key. Missteps in entering the commercial markets can be costly in terms of reputation and time lost as well as revenue. The TMT must develop a clear, comprehensive execution strategy—identify the top market opportunities, which markets to pursue first, what services to offer, resources required, strategic acquisitions, and so forth—and install the IMP.
2. *Do these aspects serve as a unique catalyst for thought leadership and strategic action?* Yes/somewhat, but extreme caution
   - These are the people who will make the strategy and mission happen. They must understand the larger mission and be involved in developing and carrying out the details of the implementation and execution.

C. Action strategy (Goals, objectives, programs, projects) T-0

1. *Do these elements serve as a unique catalyst and focus for thought leadership and strategic action?* Yes
   - Specific goals, objectives, and projects are identified and implemented for each business unit, with the IMP as overarching process.
2. *Can the rest of the firm articulate these elements of action?* Somewhat
   - Limited to corporate HQ and select field positions; most field personnel do not have a clear understanding beyond their individual unit focus.
   - Field personnel carry out the projects and objectives vs. gaining a strategic understanding.
   - Most field personnel are treated like contracted workers; there is little employee loyalty to the corporation.

C. Action strategy (Goals, objectives, programs, projects) T-5

1. *Do these elements serve as a unique catalyst and focus for thought leadership and strategic action?* Yes
   - Specific projects, goals, and objectives must be identified, developed, and implemented for each business area.
2. *Can the rest of the firm articulate these elements of action?* Yes, but caution
   - Employees must buy in and be involved to make this significant strategy a reality.

D. Reengineering (Process improvement) T-0

1. *Does this focus serve as a unique catalyst for thought leadership and strategic action?* Yes
   - TMT has established core process improvement programs to improve value and reduce costs.
   - To augment and leverage in-house resources, the TMT is expanding capabilities through Inter-divisional Work Authorizations.
2. *Can the rest of the firm articulate the reengineering focus?* Yes/Somewhat
   - Field personnel may not be able to articulate the continuous improvement/process innovation strategy.
   - Required training courses for process improvement are established for all areas.
   - Customers pay for continuous skills training to maintain leading-edge capabilities.

D. Reengineering (Process improvement) T-5

1. *Does this focus serve as a unique catalyst for thought leadership and strategic action?* Somewhat
   - The quality strategies that satisfy the U.S. government will not necessarily meet the needs and expectations of commercial customers. The TMT must lead the development of new processes and improvement methods to satisfy these new markets.
2. *Can the rest of the firm articulate the reengineering focus?* Yes
   - As ABC moves away from providing a homogeneous service to a more diverse customer-focused approach, employees at lower levels must be enlisted in creating improved service processes.

E. Key emerging topics (Technology, accounting standard changes, regulatory challenges) T-0

1. *Do these topics serve as a unique catalyst and focus for thought leadership and strategic action?* Yes
   - Based on well established corporate policies and government regulations (e.g., mandated drug testing).
   - Outsourcing based on make/buy, cost/profit/ benefit analysis.
2. *Can the rest of the firm articulate key emerging topics?* Yes/Somewhat
   - Limited to corporate HQ and select field positions, most field personnel do not have a clear understanding beyond their individual unit focus.

E. Key emerging topics (Technology, accounting standard changes, regulatory challenges) T-5

1. *Do these topics serve as a unique catalyst and focus for thought leadership and strategic action?* Yes
   - Nongovernmental markets will allow a more tailored approach to these policy areas. Cost savings could be realized as a result of new freedoms for restructuring/ reengineering certain processes, such as outsourcing, budgeting requirements, reporting.
2. *Can the rest of the firm articulate key emerging topics?* Yes/Somewhat
   - Those involved in the commercial markets may have to be educated on the new policies that apply.

7. Organizational Effectiveness System

This system includes solutions to structure, processes, climate and culture, recognition, reward, and people. The firm's "genetic code" is located in this module, and deep barriers can reside here.

Organizational Effectiveness T-0	**Organizational Effectiveness T-5**
1. *Are strategy, structure, people, rewards, processes, climate, and culture useful?* Yes/Somewhat • Strategy, structure, and processes are closely aligned with customer requirements in identified business areas. • Climate and culture reflect customer (primarily U.S. government/military) climate and culture, particularly since service operations are conducted on customer sites. • Rewards are based on achieving defined Acceptable Quality Levels and other measurable criteria; for example, employee of the month, parking privileges, scholarships for children, promotions based on leadership and competence. 2. *Are strategy, structure, people, rewards, processes, climate, and culture aligned?* Yes • Aligned to achieve customer requirements. • Aligned to assimilate within customer environments. 3. *Which structures are not useful?* None. 4. *Which parts are not aligned?* None. 5. *What barriers prevent the parts of the structure from being useful and aligned?* Not applicable	1. *Are strategy, structure, people, rewards, processes, climate, and culture useful?* Yes, with extreme caution • Strategy, structure, processes must be closely aligned with customer requirements in all of the current and newly identified business areas. • Climate and culture will be an area of significant change and challenge. Climate and culture will have to adapt to the new marketplace realities. Government-oriented culture will not match to many commercial customer cultures. • A new rewards system will have to be developed and tailored to non-U.S. government markets. ABC will have to develop criteria for rewards in the many areas where customer criteria will not be provided. 2. *Are the parts of the current structure aligned?* Yes • Aligned to achieving defined customer requirements. • Aligned to assimilate within new customer environments. 3. *Which structures are not useful?* Success depends on all being useful. 4. *Which parts are not aligned?* To be successful, all must be aligned; but this represents a significant challenge in pursuit of nontraditional markets. 5. *What barriers prevent the parts of the structure from being useful and aligned?* Not applicable

8. Drivers of Sustainable Competitive Advantage

These drivers represent the root causes for a firm's current performance level.

Relative to your best competitor, list the drivers that help to provide superior thought leadership and control customer or product platform opportunities and/or current market power position. T-0	Relative to your best competitor, list the drivers that help to provide superior thought leadership and control customer or product platform opportunities and/or current market power position. T-5
• *Transformation process drivers*—ABC has already implemented some aspects of the transformation from being mostly a DOD contractor to commercializing services. Being part of our parent corporation (XYZ) supports this effort.	• *R&D drivers*—Although ABC is moving into new opportunities, it has a strong competence in developing solutions to specific customer needs on a project-by-project basis.
• *Structure drivers*—Compared to our best competitor (a private company), ABC can maintain or make structure transitions easier through its network of divisions and corporate support.	• *Structure drivers*—ABC knows how to structure for project success. There is a strong team-based culture.
• *Network structure drivers*—ABC maintains strong inter-corporate and external communications networks that are leveraged to compete in the marketplace.	• *Network structure drivers*—The company will continue to develop and leverage its strong inter-corporate and external communications networks.
• *Strategic information system drivers*—ABC is supported by one of the most technologically advanced corporate parents in the defense industry. Information systems drive a highly sophisticated communications network utilized by all divisions.	• *Strategic information system drivers*—ABC has a strong foundation enabler of its communication network structure from its parent. It will continue to be developed as a competitive advantage.
• *Total quality management drivers*—Compared to our best competitor, ABC is able to draw on a vast amount of talent and knowledge from other divisions to complement project level and corporate quality management.	• *Command of input resources drivers*—The parent has a mature, efficient system for applying its resources effectively to carry out projects. The discipline of meeting government requirements continues to help sustain this advantage. The company will have to adapt to new freedoms and opportunities for more flexible approaches.
• *Total customer service drivers*—ABC offers many customer service drivers through access to our overall corporate capabilities and industry contacts.	

Relative to the best competitor, list those drivers that detract from providing superior thought leadership and control of customer or product platforms and/or current market power position. T-0

- *Marketing drivers*—Compared to our best competitor, ABC bids many more projects and therefore spreads marketing dollars over a larger base. Our leading competitor is able to spend large sums on fewer projects making it more difficult to compete on those specific projects.
- *New product process drivers*—ABC creates very few new products as such. This is not currently an area of emphasis in ABC's strategic plan.
- *R&D drivers*—ABC only performs R&D at a local project level. These R&D skills are transferable to the commercial world.
- *Culture drivers*—Compared to our best drivers this is one of our weakest areas. It is extremely difficult as a publicly traded corporation to create a worthwhile culture in the defense industry. Our best competitor is a privately held company, considerably smaller in size and able to enact programs that would violate laws if applied to ABC.

Relative to the best competitor, list those drivers that detract from providing superior thought leadership and control of customer or product platforms and/or current market power position. T-5

- *Marketing drivers*—There are already competitors in the commercial arena that have a strong marketing presence that ABC will have to overcome.
- *New product process drivers*—This is a new area of focus for ABC. Some move up the learning curve will be required.
- *Transformation process drivers*—In five years good progress is expected in moving forward in the transformation process, but the process will still be ongoing with many struggles and challenges.
- *People drivers*—New approaches will have to be developed to establish new compensation, reward, relationship, culture policies that align with commercial realities.
- *Compensation drivers*—Alternatives to strict government guidelines will have to be developed.
- *Culture drivers*—The big hurdle. Moving from a U.S. government defense culture to a nongovernment culture will require significant paradigms shifts. Ways of operating and even communicating (language, terms, mannerisms, etc.) will have to change. We may need outside assistance/consulting.
- *Total Quality Management drivers*—ABC has a strong basis for executing projects to meet requirements, but it will have to learn to identify satisfaction drivers for its new customers and execute new strategies to delight its new customers.
- *Total customer service drivers*—Same challenges as TQM.

Relative to the best competitor, list those drivers that are at parity for providing superior thought leadership and control of customer or product platforms and/or current market power position. T-0	**Relative to the best competitor, list those drivers that are at parity for providing superior thought leadership and control of customer or product platforms and/or current market power position. T-5**
• *People drivers*—Compared to our best competitor, ABC offers about the same people drivers. This area is constrained by government regulations, which effectively equalizes the playing field. • *Compensation drivers*—Compared to our best competitor, ABC offers about the same compensation drivers. This area is also constrained by government regulations, which equalizes the playing field.	This section remains the same as with time period T-0.

9. Maximization of Shareholder/Owner Wealth Game Board

All of the previous modules are evaluated in this module for their contribution to the firm's ability to earn more than its required rate of return.

Drivers of Owner Wealth (Sales growth rate, operating profit margin, income tax rate, incremental working capital investment, incremental fixed capital investment, required rate of return on equity, sustainability/duration of all) T-0	Drivers of Owner Wealth (Sales growth rate, operating profit margin, income tax rate, incremental working capital investment, incremental fixed capital investment, required rate of return on equity, sustainability/duration of all) T-5
1. *List the value drivers that have been and are expected to continue improving.* All • Despite, or as a result of, declining defense budgets, the company has the opportunity to take advantage of outsourcing by the government and maintenance of aging aircraft and facilities. 2. *List the value drivers that have been and are expected to continue faltering.* None 3. *Is there a useful blend of entrepreneurial spirit and the control of risk and uncertainty?* Somewhat • Limited opportunities for entrepreneurship due to confined market arena. • Well established approach to defining and controlling risk and uncertainty in the government bidding process.	1. *List the value drivers that have been and are expected to continue improving.* • Sales growth rate—Matching ABC's competencies with many new market opportunities will assure continued sales growth rate. • Operating Profit Margin— Commercial opportunities will provide higher profit margins compared with government restricted margins. • Sustainability/Duration—Expanding market opportunities will provide for sustainable growth. 2. *List the value drivers that have been and are expected to continue faltering.* • Incremental Working Capital Investment—More capital investment per sales will be required at the five-year mark as part of preparations to service new markets. • Incremental Fixed Capital Investment—U.S. government provided fixed capital facilities. Commercial customers can be expected to require ABC to invest in fixed capital to meet service needs. • Required Rate of Return on Equity—Commercial market ventures will require a higher rate of return on equity to satisfy risk and investor expectations. 3. *Is there a useful blend of entrepreneurial spirit and the control of risk and uncertainty?* Somewhat

	• This is an area of challenge. Entrepreneurship will have to become a valued attribute within ABC to aggressively pursue market opportunities and satisfy diverse customer needs. • The company is moving into a more uncertain environment in pursuing commercial ventures. The ability to move quickly and change/adapt will be keys to success in this environment.

10. Entrepreneurial Strategy Development Process

The process lays a foundation that ensures that all the requirements necessary for successfully competing in the future are made available to the TMT and other opinion leaders and process champions in a timely, user friendly, and value added manner.

A. System format, calendar, specific deliverables T-0	A. System format, calendar, specific deliverables T-5

1. *Does a useful plan exist for these factors that is consistent with the other modules?* Yes/Somewhat
  • Spring and Fall strategic planning sessions driven by TMT.
  • Specific plans developed for each area: general managers, then financial/contract/admin, then operations, then HR, then all are brought together to view the corporate-wide plan.
  • Same questions and format for each group are provided by the strategic planning department to provide consistency and framework for blending strategies among the areas.
2. *Which plans are useful and value added?*
  • Most useful is blending of the strategies for integrated corporate-wide strategic approach.
3. *Which plans are not useful and add no value?*
  • Lack of cross-functional approach to initially develop strategic plans for each functional area; often must contend with conflicts among submitted functional plans.
	1. *Does a useful plan exist for these factors that is consistent with the other modules?* Yes/Somewhat
	  • Strategic planning sessions driven by TMT will provide the forum for establishing specific plans and deliverables for developing and implementing the new strategy.
	  • The planning process for functional areas will have to adapt to address commercial projects. This will require a shift in thinking from the mindset of a yearly government process.
	2. *Which plans are useful and value added?*
	  • The strategic planning process will still be a useful solution, with adaptations for commercial projects.

B. Decision/approval processes T-0
1. *Does a useful plan exist for these factors that is consistent with the other modules?* Yes
  • Controlled process due to nature of government contract environment.
2. *Which plans are useful and value added?*
  • Controlled process due to nature of government contract environment.
	B. Decision/approval processes T-5
	1. *Does a useful plan exist for these factors that is consistent with the other modules?* Yes
	  • The entire system must be consistent.
	2. *Which plans are useful and value added?*
	  • All plans must be useful and add value.

2. *Which plans are useful and value added?*
   - Controlled approval process to assure compliance and defined corporate strategy.
   - Checks and balances among areas part of TMT approval process.
   - Provides focus for the TMT and the corporation.
   - Interaction within units to develop decisions on strategic requests.
3. *Which plans are not useful and add no value?*
   - Lack of cross-functional approach at lower levels.

3. *Which plans are not useful and add no value?*
   - Too centralized to address fast-paced, tailored commercial projects.
   - Empowerment of appropriate levels will be required to meet customers' specific needs within a time-intensive competitive environment.
   - Interactions within units to develop decisions on strategic requests will be a significant challenge. Functional units will have to be more flexible.

C. Inter-accountabilities T-0

1. *Does a useful plan exist for these factors that is consistent with the other modules?* Yes
2. *Which plans are useful and value added?*
   - Strategic planning approach does foster some cross-functional cooperation.
3. *Which plans are not useful and add no value?*
   - Cross-functional coordination is by necessity instead of part of a defined approach to coordination among units at lower levels.

C. Inter-accountabilities T-5

1. *Does a useful plan exist for these factors that is consistent with the other modules?* Yes
2. *Which plans are useful and value added?*
   - Strategic planning approach does foster some cross-functional cooperation—but needs to improve dramatically.
3. *Which plans are not useful and add no value?*
   - Cross-functional coordination needs to be enabled by the Initiative Management Process and discipline.

D. Resource allocation process T-0

1. *Does a useful plan exist for these factors that is consistent with the other modules?* Yes
2. *Which plans are useful and value added?*
   - Established resource allocation system based on key word search.
   - Financial allocations conducted yearly with mid-year adjustments.
   - Team approach used to achieve consensus at all levels.
3. *Which plans are not useful and add no value?*
   - Functional adversarial realtionships.
   - Power plays among managers.

D. Resource allocation process T-5
This whole section remains the same as with time period T-0.

E. Budgeting process and system T-0	**E. Budgeting process and system T-5**
1. *Does a useful plan exist for these factors that is consistent with the other modules?* Yes/Somewhat	This whole section remains the same as with time period T-0.
2. *Which plans are useful and value added?* • Clear guidelines and cost controls. • Aligned with customer cost visibility. • Balance volume, business enhancement, performance efficiencies, and positive cash flows. • Bottom-up budgeting based on documented constraints—empowers individual managers.	
3. *Which plans are not useful and add no value?* • Arbitrary cuts often made across the board. • You can be "punished" by cuts if you are honest and don't "sandbag" the budget.	

11. High Performance Team Chalkboard

This last module allows a company to come together as a Team of High Performance Teams with focus, clarity, direction, energy, and leadership.

A. Foundation/visibility/power T-0
1. *Do you have a way of ensuring team power and visibility consistent with the needs of modules 1–10?* Yes
2. *Which methods are useful?*
  • Foundation for teamwork is based on established projects—provides clear team focus on project goals, measurements, etc.
  • Power and visibility based on size and risk of project.
  • Availability of corporate parent resources to apply to projects.
  • Large pool of knowledgeable resources from which to draw effective team strength.
3. *Which methods are not useful?*
  • Geographic dispersion and diverse scope/nature of projects are major challenges for effective corporate wide teamwork.
	A. Foundation/visibility/power T-5
	This whole section remains the same as with time period T-0.

B. Correct number of teams T-0
1. *Do you have a way of creating the optimal number of teams required by modules 1–10?* Yes
  • Ten major projects in building blocks in place.
2. *Which methods are useful?*
  • Project approach brings together cross-functional resources focused on achieving common goals.
3. *Which methods are not useful?*
  • Some organizational silo effect from both project and functional standpoints; can impede effective application of resources across organizational and project boundaries.
	B. Correct number of teams T-5
	This whole section remains the same as with time period T-0.

C. Team makeup T-0	**C. Team makeup T-5**
1. *Do you have a way of creating teams with the make-up required by modules 1–10?* Yes	This whole section remains the same as with time period T-0.
2. *Which methods are useful?*	
• Cross-functional approach and support.	
• Strong base of expertise.	
• Team membership based on availability and volunteers.	
3. *Which methods are not useful?*	
• Sometimes overkill in number and types of people and organizations brought in to participate on the project can reduce team effectiveness and cycle time.	
D. Readiness to be a team T-0	**D. Readiness to be a team T-5**
1. *Do you have a way of ensuring team readiness as required by modules 1–10?* Somewhat	This whole section remains the same as with time period T-0.
2. *Which methods are useful?*	
• Project team approach is part of the culture.	
3. *Which methods are not useful?*	
• Organization silo and competition issues among units and projects.	
• Competing agendas.	
• Some conflict between established and progressive ideas.	
E. Ways to provide interconnectedness among teams T-0	**E. Ways to provide interconnectedness among teams T-5**
1. *Do you have a way of interconnecting teams as required by modules 1–10?* Somewhat	This whole section remains the same as with time period T-0.
2. *Which methods are useful?*	
• Common project responsibilities and goals.	
3. *Which methods are not useful?*	
• Problems sharing information among functional areas.	
• Sometimes projects/functions do not see opportunities to leverage corporate resources—shortsighted.	

F. Ways to measure team performance T-0	**F. Ways to measure team performance T-5**
1. *Do you have a useful way of measuring team performance in modules 1–10?* Somewhat 2. *Which methods are useful?* • Clearly established measurements and requirements based on contractual agreements. 3. *Which methods are not useful?* • Measures can inhibit cross-functional teamwork. "Why apply my resources if the success of that organization or project is not tied to my performance measurement?"	This whole section remains the same as with time period T-0.

ABC's key customers purchased about every 18 to 24 months, creating a market rhythm of about every 4 to 5 months. Using the formula introduced in Chapter 8, we determined that mega-burst changes would occur within 4 to 8 months (one to two market rhythms) while micro-burst changes would be felt within 12 to 25 months (three to five market rhythms). As the plan was played out, every one of the eleven modules experienced significant change that caused mega-burst and micro-burst changes throughout the system.

For example, in 1997 (the second year out in the rolling plan), unconventional outsourcing competitors began entering ABC's industry by bidding in Requests for Proposals from ABC's customers. The change was in Module 1 (The Stadium), especially within sub-module A that addresses current industry trajectory and being under attack by a well-financed/strong competitor. Within four months, the mega-burst change predictably occurred in the firm's strategic financial paradigm (Module 2), as frequent heated discussions began about the required tier size and assets/fixed costs. Then micro-burst changes reached Module 4—Customer Intimacy, Loyalty and Profitability Profile (Were customers abandoning ABC or just playing their cards?); Module 6—Strategy in Fives (Would the seeming ease with which new entrants were bidding foretell a need for change in grand strategy?); Module 8—Drivers of Sustainable Competitive Advantage (Would the "shape of ABC's strategy need to change quickly and, if so, would a new "dominant logic" need to be conceived with different drivers?); and Module 10—Entrepreneurial Strategy Development Process (Would an advance team need to be fielded to develop a total new strategy and planning process to fend off these new entrants?). These micro-burst changes happened simultaneously at about one year after the change in the environment became widely known—on the short side of the 12- to 24-month rule of thumb.

In that same year (1997), the corporate parent changed its commitment and sought more cash from ABC to help fund other corporate initiatives. This change affected the firm's strategic financial paradigm (Module 2), and was a huge blow to the strategic direction ABC had established. Cash the firm had counted on was no longer available. Again, the mega-burst and micro-burst changes in other parts of the organization occurred in predictable fashion.

The ABC team did not get everything right nor did they do everything perfectly. But what they did, they did well enough to succeed and to continue moving toward becoming the defining entity in their industry. The plan was updated on a rolling, five-year schedule: When a new year was added to the scenario, the most recent year was dropped off. As 2000 approached as the current year, the analysis was strengthened because of access to more accurate information, but by then, the five-year vision had been extended to 2005. A dynamic strategic planning process with a rolling, five-year plan, combined with early warning signals from the mega- and micro-burst ripples of change, blends formulation and execution and incorporates data from cycles of learning that are gained through success and failure.

A strategy execution lens helps everyone to recognize that nothing is ever perfect. There is only the opportunity to improve, to learn, and to build a platform of success and confidence so that bolder initiatives can be pursued. Making mistakes is human and inevitable. We must purge from our thinking and our language the notion that "excellence" is the same as "perfection." The concepts and tools presented here and in Chapter 8 are some of the most complex in the book. But if a team of executives can engage these ideas, they can have an almost immediate impact on improving the organization's dynamic strategic planning, scenario building, and change management.

Epilogue: Not long ago, XYZ was purchased by an even larger defense technology firm, and ABC's units were dispersed among the business units of the new owner. The value of ABC was a key component of the overall purchase price, in large part because of its strategy execution prowess. This epilogue reminds us that nothing stays the same in the business world—just one more reason why world-class strategy execution skills are now, and will continue to be, a key source of competitive advantage and value creation.

Appendix 4

A Mini-Diagnostic Survey: Assessing Your Company's Track Record in Initiative Management and Innovation and Growth Strategies

This mini-diagnostic survey is designed to assess a company's current status in strategy execution. Much of what can be diagnosed about the performance of a company can be learned by assessing how well it executes the major initiatives that come out of its strategic management process.

Initiatives are the key pieces of work that are expected to directly increase the market value of the firm. These initiatives can be strategic, operating, or support in nature. At any given time, a firm will probably have a portfolio of initiatives that are in various stages of completion—ongoing, stalled, terminated, "secret," new, or under consideration. Completed initiatives will almost always find a home within the maintenance work of the firm—the day-to-day work being done in functions, processes, geographic areas, and the corporate center that keeps the organization going.

Most of a firm's problems in initiative management arise from one or more of four types: subject matter barriers, process barriers, structure barriers, and culture barriers.

- *Subject matter barriers* are related to disagreements among key players in an industry, such as determining standards for a new technology, choosing to be an industry leader or follower, or cannibalizing a current channel for a new channel.

- *Process barriers* are impediments that cause longer cycle time, more rework, or increased costs in the portfolio of executive, operating, and support processes. Examples include ineffective measures of portfolio performance, poor process design, and changing priorities.

- *Structure barriers* are caused by a lack of fit between the structural basis of the firm—organizing by product, customer, technology, or geographic area—and the market and customer interfaces required to keep pace with faster market rhythms. These barriers create problems within themselves and can, in turn, cause many process barriers.

• *Culture barriers* are executive biases, blind spots, and faulty mental models that cause inertia, delay, disastrous decisions, inappropriate resource allocation, political infighting, and chronic anxiety and fatigue that diminish the organization's courage and resolve.

Please complete the following questionnaire. Offer as many clarifying comments as possible, as they help to identify current assumptions. There are no right or wrong answers, only the reality of the situation your company is currently facing.

Company: _____

Your position: _____

Years with the company: _____

Years in this position: _____

Phone: _____

Email: _____

1. Describe your company's strategy execution process. Check one of the following choices:

❑ Process is not yet developed.
❑ Process is not well defined or shared.
❑ Process is well defined, but shared only with a small group.
❑ Process is clear for a small group, but not well communicated to the larger group.
❑ Process is clear with near universal understanding.

Briefly describe how your formulated strategies are executed to timely, measurable results.

_____

_____

_____

_____

Comment on how well this process is working now and changes that could make it work better.

_____

_____

_____

_____

_____

2. Mark the point on each continuum that describes your company's position at the present time.

  A. The strategy implementation process responds to and prioritizes the correct new opportunities or initiatives.

Never		**Sometimes**		**Always**
X	X	X	X	X

  B. Everyone in the organization understands the strategies and the portfolio of initiatives produced from the process.

Never		**Sometimes**		**Always**
X	X	X	X	X

  C. Everyone in the organization can adequately describe the strategy and the portfolio of initiatives.

Never		**Sometimes**		**Always**
X	X	X	X	X

Comment on how well this process is working now and changes that could make it work better.

_____

_____

_____

_____

_____

_____

_____

_____

_____

_____

_____

_____

_____

_____

_____

_____

_____

3. List your major initiatives. For each initiative, indicate the name of its prime
   mover, its status (on schedule, stalled, reformulated) and the barriers it faces.

	Initiative	**Prime Mover**	**Status**	**Barriers**
1.				
2.				
3.				
4.				
5.				
6.				
7.				
8.				
9.				
10.				

4. Describe your company's track record of success in implementing its growth
   initiatives to timely, measurable results. Check one of the following choices:

   ❑ Almost all initiatives have failed to meet timing and financial results.
   ❑ About 25% of the initiatives have met timing and financial results.
   ❑ About 50% of the initiatives have met timing and financial results.
   ❑ About 75% of the initiatives have met timing and financial results.
   ❑ About 95% of the initiatives have met timing and financial results; some have done
     so at world-class speeds. We have captured critical learning from these actions.

Comment on how well this process is working now and changes that could
make it work better.

5. Mark the point on the continuum that describes your company's method of identifying and selecting new initiatives to help the company achieve its growth and innovation objectives.

SBU Presidents Suggest and Are Accountable		A Combination of Both Methods		An Overarching Process Oversees All Growth Initiatives Always
X	X	X	X	X

Comment on how well this process is working now and changes that could
make it work better.

_____

_____

_____

_____

_____

_____

_____

6. Mark a point on the continuum that describes the major capabilities your company needs in order to succeed.

Functional and Process in Nature		A Comination of Both		Entrepreneurial and Customer Realtionship in Nature
X	X	X	X	X

Would most people in your company agree with your assessment?

_____

Comment on how well your current capabilities match those you need and
changes that may have to be made.

7. Describe what most people in your company think about the fit between the organization's culture and the drive for growth and innovation. Check one of the following choices:

☐ Innovation and growth imperatives do not fit with the current culture.

☐ Innovation and growth happen sometimes, but change champions usually do not receive real commitment, and the attempt fades away.

☐ Innovation and growth initiatives are funded, but they are not reviewed within a specific growth process and tend to be absorbed in routine reviews of unit performance.

☐ Innovation and growth happen in surges—when someone has a hot idea that is funded—but there is no process to ensure growth on a regular basis.

☐ A smoothly running innovation and growth process connects opportunities with the right funding and the right people at the right time, and is linked and synchronized with other executive and operating processes of the firm.

Comment on how well the culture is adjusting to growth demands and changes that could allow the culture to better accommodate growth.

_____

_____

_____

_____

_____

8. Describe how well your company understands its major stakeholders' expectations regarding innovation and growth. Check one of the following choices:

☐ We are unclear about expectations.

☐ We have begun within the last two years to assess expectations.

☐ We are responsive to stakeholders' expectations, but do not influence them proactively.

☐ We have knowledge of, are responsive to, and seek to influence stakeholders' expectations.

☐ About 95% of the time, we strongly influence stakeholders' current and future expectations regarding innovation and growth.

Comment on the effectiveness of your process for assessing stakeholder expectations and changes that could make it work better.

_____

_____

_____

_____

9. Describe your company's innovation and growth history and its success in terms of breakeven on investment and increasing shareholder wealth. Check one of the following choices:

❑ We have just begun and have no history of success.

❑ We have had spurts of innovation and growth, but a poor track record of success—one in ten initiatives breaks even on investment.

❑ We have had limited success—33%–50% of our initiatives break even on investment.

❑ Innovation and growth are part of our culture—initiatives break even 75% of the time, and half of them ultimately earn their required ROR and increase shareholder wealth.

❑ We enjoy solid innovation and growth performance—initiatives break even 95% of the time and earn their required ROR and increase shareholder wealth.

Comment on the effectiveness of your performance management process and changes that could make it work better.

_____

_____

_____

_____

_____

_____

_____

_____

_____

_____

10. Describe the degree to which barriers have inhibited your company's success in strategic innovation and growth. Check one of the following choices:

❑ Culture, structure, and process barriers interfere throughout the company and have produced deeply ingrained biases that blind people to reality.

❑ Culture and process barriers exist in many places; efforts to eliminate them are successful 10%–25% of the time.

❑ Culture and process barriers exist, but are neutralized about 50% of the time; structural barriers are dealt with as required.

❑ Few structure, culture, and process barriers exist, we experience industry subject matter barriers, but are able to gain consensus on these issues about 75% of the time.

❑ The uncertainties around industry subject matter issues are our only barrier, and they are always removed quickly through study and team agreement.

Comment on the effectiveness of your process for barrier identification and removal and changes that could make it work better.

_____

_____

_____

_____

_____

_____

_____

_____

11. Describe the biggest threats or challenges to your company's strategic innovation and growth success. Check one of the following choices:

❏ We have deep strategy formulation and implementation barriers with numerous blind spots; we do a terrible job of integrating our acquisitions; and our structure continues to inhibit any action on good ideas.

❏ We try to implement, but initiatives are frequently delayed because we are too internally oriented, too rigidly structured in functional silos, and too reactive, and we have our share of formulation and implementation barriers.

❏ We have some culture and process barriers, the beginnings of a process, and a cross-functional team mindset; about 50% of our initiatives are implemented on time and with desired results, and we are in the process of neutralizing structure barriers.

❏ We have few culture and process barriers and our processes, cross-functional teams, and project management are taken seriously; we implement with success 75% of the time.

❏ Our only real threats are our competitors' actions for which we have good responses 95% of the time; we know how to identify and choose new initiatives, deal with industry issues, and implement with world-class skill.

Comment on the effectiveness of your process for anticipating and responding to threats and new challenges and changes that could make the process work better.

_____

_____

_____

_____

_____

_____

_____

12. Describe your company's performance on maintenance work.

	Way below expectations		As expected		Beyond expectations
1. In its functions	X	X	X	X	X
2. In its processes	X	X	X	X	X
3. In its business units	X	X	X	X	X
4. In the geographical areas	X	X	X	X	X
5. In the corporate center	X	X	X	X	X

Comment on how well your capabilities for performing beyond expectations match your needs and the changes that could make the process work better.

_____

_____

_____

13. Describe the present nature and climate of your company's overall culture. Check one choice in each of the following groups:

❏ Extremely rigid.
❏ Somewhat rigid.
❏ Neither.
❏ Somewhat flexible.
❏ Extremely flexible.

❏ Extremely isolated.
❏ Somewhat isolated.
❏ Neither.
❏ Somewhat externally focused.
❏ Extremely externally focused.

❏ Extremely cautious.
❏ Somewhat cautious.
❏ Neither.
❏ Somewhat risk taking.
❏ Extremely risk taking.

❏ Extremely close-minded.
❏ Somewhat close-minded
❏ Neither.
❏ Somewhat open-minded.
❏ Extremely open-minded.

❏ Extremely reactive.
❏ Somewhat reactive.
❏ Neither.
❏ Somewhat proactive.
❏ Extremely proactive.

Scoring. For all questions except No. 4 and No. 5, score the top choice as a 1 and scale up to 5 for the bottom choice; for continuums from left to right, score the left-most choice as a 1 and scale up to 5 for the right-most choice. For questions No. 4 and No. 5, the center position indicating a combination of both methods, is scored a 5; the position on the far left of center scores a 1 and the position next to it scores a 2; the position on the far right scores a 4 and the position between center and the right scores a 3. Using this formula, sum to calculate your total score. Your score will indicate an initial placement on two matrixes: the Growth and Innovation Grid and the Learning Curriculum Matrix. Together these baseline results will serve as discussion-starters for your company's management team.

The following score ranges indicate the most likely starting place for your innovation and growth journey as described on the Growth and Innovation Grid shown below. As you will note, there is an overlap in the interpretation of scores for the Bigger and Broader quadrants. Choosing between these options will depend on top management assessment of the answers given to the open-ended questions.

Score	Starting Place for Growth and Innovation
22-44	*Getting Better Quadrant.* Strategies include aligning capacities and processes, cultivating preferences, propagating usage, and dominating the market.
45-67	*Getting Bigger Quadrant:* Strategies include extending/adding on to offerings, replicating businesses, adapting approaches for diversity, and expanding globally.
59-90	*Getting Broader Quadrant.* Strategies include managing life cycle succession, accompanying customers, inventing alternatives for customers, and launching innovations.
91-110	*Getting Bolder Quadrant.* Strategies include pursuing previously inaccessible opportunities, preempting competition, creating whole new businesses, becoming a defining entity.

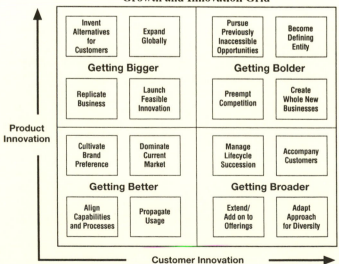

Growth and Innovation Grid

The following score ranges indicate the most likely starting place for your innovation and growth journey as described on the Learning Curriculum Matrix shown below. As in the scoring above, there is an overlap in the interpretation of scores for reengineering and top line growth. Again, choosing between these options will depend on top management assessment of the answers given to the open-ended questions.

Score	Starting Place for Growth and Innovation
22-23	Turnaround management mix of education, training, expert panels, commissioned studies, and so forth.
34-45	Cost reduction mix.
46-70	Reengineering mix for executive, operating, and support processes.
65-90	Mix of rapid top line growth initiatives with no new net investment.
91-110	Mix of breakthrough opportunities.

Learning Curriculum Matrix

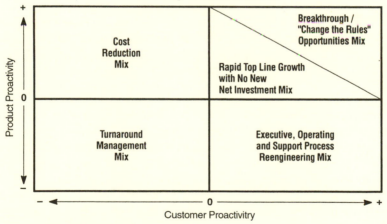

"+", "0" and "–" are relative to best competitor

Glossary

This Glossary groups terms in two categories: (1) models and frameworks of the New Science and (2) key definitions. It is designed to offer a quick review of the entire New Science approach to strategy execution, as well as to clarify the terms. The chapter references relate to the place in the book in which the topics are discussed in more detail.

THE MODELS AND FRAMEWORKS OF THE NEW SCIENCE

Six Forces That Are Changing Business: Globalization, industry convergence, electronic commerce, innovation and growth, disruptive technology, and fading customer loyalty (Chapter 1).

The Five Aspects of the New Science: Five modular elements that sum to produce world-class strategy execution: Aspect 1. The Initiative Management Process (Chapter 4); Aspect 2. Executive, Operating, and Support Processes Becoming PALS with Market Rhythms (Chapter 5); Aspect 3. The Growth and Innovation Roadmap (Chapter 6); Aspect 4. The Timing of Four Competitive Thrusts (Chapter 7); and Aspect 5. Managing Mega- and Micro-Burst Ripple Effects (Chapter 9).

The Four Key Competitive Thrusts: Initiatives for growth, process reengineering and improvement, controllable cost reduction, and turnaround management must be timed to fit within the appropriate competitive environment (Chapter 7).

The Seven Stages of Growth and Continuous Improvement: Stage 1. Vision and Inspiration; Stage 2. Focus and Control; Stage 3. Growth; Stage 4. Process Redesign and Improvement; Stage 5. Product/Cost Optimization; Stage 6. Revisioning and Wealth Creation; Stage 7. Strengthening the Foundation for the Next Plateau (Chapter 6). These typical stages can help a firm map its growth and continuous improvement journey.

The Six Transition Phases Between the Seven Stages of Growth and Continuous Improvement: The degradation of one stage gives rise to a transition phase, which propels the firm to the next stage of growth and continuous improvement (Chapter 6).

Magnanimity and Integrity in the Seven Stages: A concept of organizational health and effectiveness that stresses prudence and foresight in leading and managing, and consistency with the demands of both the current and next stages of growth (Chapter 6).

The 10 S's: A new look at the McKinsey 7-S model of the 1980s, updated for the demands of business in the 21st century (Chapter 3).

The 4 Bs: Getting better, getting bigger, getting broader, getting bolder (Chapter 4).

The Nine Steps in the Product Line Innovation Process and Their Barriers: Step 1. Cycles of Information (COI) (COI Barriers); Step 2. New Product/Service Creativity (Creativity Barriers); Step 3. Tacit/Explicit Knowledge Subprocesses (Knowledge Barriers); Step 4. Innovation (Innovation Barriers); Step 5. Innovation Accelerated by Resource Capability (Resource Capability Barriers); Step 6. Design/Development Process (D/D Process Barriers); Step 7. Launched Products and Services; Step 8. Learning From Launch (Barriers to Learning); Step 9. Building Successful Innovation Platforms (Chapter 10).

The Four Phases of the Initiative Management Process (IMP): Phase 1. Generation; Phase 2. Commitment; Phase 3. Development/Implementation; Phase 4. Realization (Chapter 4).

Gates Between the Phases of the IMP: Checkpoints within the IMP process for reassessing an initiative according to prioritizing criteria (Chapter 4).

The Eleven Modules of Organizational Activity That Send and Receive Ripple Effects of Change: 1. The stadium in which the firm competes; 2. Strategic financial paradigm; 3. CEO/top management team roles; 4. Customer intimacy, loyalty, and profitability profile; 5. Communicating with customers through strategic marketing; 6. Strategy in fives; 7. Organizational effectiveness system; 8. Drivers of sustainable competitive advantage; 9. Maximization of owner wealth game board; 10. Entrepreneurial strategy development process; 11. High performance team chalkboard (Chapter 8).

KEY DEFINITIONS FOR THE NEW SCIENCE

AIPs: Actions in Progress (Chapter 2).

Architect Role: The responsibility for designing the organization's *form*, including structure, control systems, and information processes.

BRT: A barrier removal team—a team that has been trained to identify and remove barriers to world-class strategy execution (Chapter 9).

Buying Cycle: The frequency with which a firm's best customers buy a product or service (Chapter 3).

CFPT: A cross-functional process team—a team that is charged with improving process cycle times (Chapter 9).

Cockpit Chart: A way to display lead measures (drivers) and lag measures (results). This system works best if metrics from key units of a company are rolled up to show the total company progress and results (Chapter 9).

Cycle Time: The linear time elapsed from the beginning of a process to when its last deliverable is complete.

Cycle Time Roll Up of Executive, Operating, and Support Processes: The total cycle time of *all* supporting executive, operating, and support processes for one initiative as it progresses through the IMP (Chapter 4).

Double Loop Learning: Learning that changes the mental model that gave rise to an ineffective strategy as well as changing performance so that the strategy's actual performance can match its planned performance (Chapter 9).

Drumbeat: A weekly measure of leading measures against expectations. Measuring cycle time, percent of rework, and cost weekly and reporting monthly emphasizes process discipline, which is crucial for world-class strategy execution (Chapter 9).

Dynamic Cycle Time: A measure based on the total number of active AIPs in a given year divided by the number of AIPs completed (as defined by their original business cases) during the same year (Chapter 2).

Executive Process Improvement: Improving efficiency—the speed at which key initiatives are turned into outputs and results with no rework as compared to the speed of a major new entrant; improving productivity—the percentage of initiatives that hit their original performance targets with no rework as compared to the achievement of world-class, venture capital firms; improving effectiveness—the growth rate of the market value of the firm compared to the growth in market value of a successful new entrant (Chapter 2).

HPT: A high performance team that has the following attributes: participative leadership, shared responsibility, broad vision, priority focus, creativity, and rapid response (Chapter 9).

IMP: The Initiative Management Process (Chapter 4).

IOT: A cross-functional innovation opportunity team that is given "incubator" authority, accountability, and visibility.

IT: A cross-functional initiative team that leads and manages an initiative through the IMP (Chapter 9).

Lag Measures: Measures based on a process's results—sales, inventory level, margins, cash flow, customer satisfaction, stock price, and so forth (Chapter 9).

Lead Measures: Measures that indicate progress through a process—cycle time, percent of rework, and cost (Chapter 9).

Learning Time for the New Science Discipline: It will take about 25 to 30 times the market rhythm time for learning to take root before end results and other benefits can be achieved (Chapter 9).

Market Rhythm: The true underlying pulse of the market. On average this rhythm is about four to five times faster than the customer buying cycle (Chapter 3).

Market Rhythm Capture: The percent of economic profit a firm captures within a three-month period of market rhythms (Chapter 3).

Master Builder Role: The responsibility for blending together processes and people to achieve results.

Mega-Burst Impact: The effect of a major change in one part of the organization that will strongly affect another part of the organization within the space of two or three market rhythms (Chapter 8).

Micro-Burst Impact: The ripple effect of mega-burst change as it spreads to other parts of the organization, usually within three to five market rhythms (Chapter 8).

Output Rate and Financial Realization of the Initiative Management Process: The time it takes for an initiative to go through the IMP and achieve its financial results as compared to objectives set in the original business plan (Chapter 4).

PALS: Processes that are prioritized, aligned, linked, and synchronized with each other and with market rhythms (Chapter 3).

Powers-of-Three Teams: The teams responsible for oversight of the initiative teams (ITs). To ensure a system of checks and balances, these teams should be composed of at least three executives, each of whom has a different logic and mental model of the business (Chapter 9).

Process Yield: A measure of how many units of work go through a process with no rework; expressed as a percent—100% yield means no rework.

Program Office: The office that maintains oversight of the entire New Science approach; this office must be formed in every SBU of a multi-unit corporation because the New Science makes the most sense when applied at the business unit level (Chapter 9).

Response Time: The time that elapses between a customer's request and the beginning of action to satisfy the order.

Single Loop Learning: The learning that changes a strategic approach so that the actual performance of a strategy can match its planned performance (Chapter 9).

Strawman: A model, framework, or measurement approach that is sufficiently tested and useful in providing a good starting place for planning change. It prevents starting from nothing and wasting cycle time—the anathema to world-class strategy execution.

Symptoms of Dysfunction: A set of observable attributes that can suggest underlying root causes of too long cycle times, large amounts of rework, and high costs in the suite of executive, operating, and support processes (Chapter 1).

Total Cycle Time: The combined cycle times of all business processes from the point at which a need arises until it is satisfied.

Visionary Role: The responsibility for using foresight and creativity to intuitively understand the trends underlying changes in customers' buying patterns and to project the impact of those shifts on the organization.

Bibliography

The books in this bibliography are my favorites. The older books on the list have influenced my theories of organization action in many ways, and I continue to draw from them today. The diverse ideas contained in these books have given me the lenses to frame the challenges, search for root causes, and recommend strategies in the over 90 client firms I have worked with during the last two decades. The newer books are included on the list because they corroborate my thinking in the New Science of Strategy Execution. I do not agree with all of the views suggested in these materials. I offer them only because they have influenced me to confirm or reject ideas as part of the New Science.

Abell, Derek F. *Defining the Business: The Starting Point of Strategic Planning.* Englewood Cliffs, N.J.: Prentice Hall, 1980.

Adams, James L. *Conceptual Blockbusting: A Guide to Better Ideas*, 2nd ed. New York: W. W. Norton, 1979.

Adizes, Ichak. *Managing Corporate Lifecycles.* Rev. ed. of *Corporate Lifecycles.* Paramus, N.J.: Prentice Hall, 1999.

Aguayo, Rafael. *Dr. Deming: The American Who Taught the Japanese About Quality.* New York: Simon and Schuster, 1991.

Ainsworth-Land, George T. *Grow or Die: The Unifying Principle of Transformation*, 2nd ed. rev. New York: John Wiley and Sons, 1986.

Aldrich, Howard E. *Organizations and Environments.* Englewood Cliffs, N. J.: Prentice Hall, 1979.

Amran, Martha, and Nalin Kulatilaka. *Real Options: Managing Strategic Investment in an Uncertain World.* Boston: Harvard Business School Press, 1999.

Arendt, Hannah. *The Life of the Mind, Volume One—Thinking.* New York: Harcourt Brace Jovanovich, 1971.

Baghai, Mehroad, Stephen Coley, and David White. *The Alchemy of Growth: Practical Insights for Building the Enduring Enterprise.* Cambridge, Mass.: Perseus Publishing, 2000.

Barker, Joel Arthur. *Paradigms: The Business of Discovering the Future*. New York: Harper Business, 1992.

Bechtell, Michele L. *The Management Compass: Steering the Corporation Using Hoshin Planning*. New York: AMA Management Briefing, 1995.

Berry, Thomas H. *Managing the Total Quality Transformation*. New York: McGraw-Hill, 1991.

Bibeault, Donald B. *Corporate Turnaround: How Managers Turn Losers Into Winners*. New York: McGraw-Hill, 1982.

Bogue, Marcus, III, and Elwood Buffa. *Corporate Strategic Analysis*. New York: Free Press, 1986.

Bossidy, Larry, and Ram Charan. *Execution: The Discipline of Getting Things Done*. New York: Crown Business, 2002.

Burgelman, Robert A., and Leonard R. Sayles. *Inside Corporate Innovation: Strategy, Structure, and Managerial Skills*. New York: Free Press, 1986.

Burgelman, Robert A., and Modesto A. Maidique. *Strategic Management of Technology and Innovation*. Homewood, Ill.: Irwin, 1988.

Carlzon, Jan. *Moments of Truth*. Cambridge, Mass.: Ballinger Publishing, 1987.

Chandler, David G. *Atlas of Military Strategy*. New York: Free Press, 1980.

Charan, Ram, and Noel M. Tichy. *Every Business Is a Growth Business*. New York: Times Business, 1998.

Christensen, Clayton M. *The Innovator's Dilemma: When Technologies Cause Great Firms to Fail*. Boston: Harvard Business School Press, 1997.

Cleland, Alan S., and Albert V. Bruno. *The Market Value Process: Bridging Customer and Shareholder Value*. San Francisco: Jossey-Bass, 1996.

Collins, James C. *Good to Great: Why Some Companies Make the Leap . . . and Others Don't*. New York: HarperBusiness, 2001.

Daniels, Aubrey C. *Performance Management: Improving Quality Productivity Through Positive Reinforcement*. 3rd ed. rev. Tucker, Ga.: Performance Management Publications, 1989.

————. *Bringing Out the Best in People: How to Apply the Astonishing Power of Positive Reinforcement*. New York: McGraw-Hill, 1994.

Davenport, Thomas H. *Process Innovation: Reengineering Work Through Information Technology*. Boston: Harvard Business School Press, 1993.

Davis, Marvin A. *Turnaround: The No-Nonsense Guide to Corporate Renewal*. Chicago: Contemporary Books, 1987.

de Bono, Edward. *Six Thinking Hats*. Boston: Little Brown and Company, 1985.

DeGreene, Kenyon B. *The Adaptive Organization: Anticipation and Management of Crisis*. New York: Wiley Interscience, 1982.

Drucker, Peter F. *The Effective Executive*. New York: Harper and Row, 1966.

Emory, F. E., ed. *Systems Thinking: Selected Readings*. Middlesex, England: Penguin Books, 1969.

Evans, Philip, and Thomas S. Wurster. *Blown to Bits: How the New Economics of Information Transforms Strategy*. Boston: Harvard Business School Press, 2000.

Fine, Charles H. *Clockspeed: Winning Industry Control in the Age of Temporary Advantage*. Reading, Mass.: Perseus Books, 1998.

Forrester, Jay. *Industrial Dynamics*, Student's Edition, Cambridge, Mass.: MIT Press, 1961.

————. *Principles of Systems*. 2nd preliminary ed. Cambridge, Mass.: MIT Press, 1968.

Foster, Richard N. *Innovation: The Attacker's Advantage*. New York: Summit Books, 1986.

Gardner, John W. *On Leadership, with a Preface to the Paperback Edition. New York: Free Press, 1990.*

Gertz, Dwight L., and Joao P. A. Baptista. *Grow to Be Great: Breaking the Downsizing Cycle*. New York: Free Press, 1995.

Ghemawat, Pankaj. *Commitment: The Dynamics of Strategy*. New York: Free Press, 1991.

Goldratt, Eliyahu M., and Jeff Cox, *The Goal: A Process of Ongoing Improvement*. 2nd rev. ed. New York: North River Press, 1992.

———. *Critical Chain*. New York: North River Press, 1997.

Goold, Michael, Andrew Campbell, and Marcus Alexander. *Corporate-Level Strategy: Creating Value in the Multibusiness Company*. New York: John Wiley and Sons, 1994.

Hamel, Gary, and C. K. Prahalad. *Competing for the Future: Breakthrough Strategies for Seizing Control of Your Industry and Creating Markets of Tomorrow*. Boston: Harvard Business School Press, 1994.

Hamel, Gary. *Leading the Revolution*. Boston: Harvard Business School Press, 2000.

Hammer, Michael, and James Champy. *Reengineering the Corporation: A Manifesto for Business Revolution*. New York: Harper Business, 1993.

Hammermesh, Richard G. *Making Strategy Work: How Senior Managers Produce Results*. New York: John Wiley and Sons, 1986.

Hampden-Turner, Charles. *Charting the Corporate Mind: Graphic Solutions to Business Conflicts*. New York: Free Press, 1990.

Harrington, H. James. *The Improvement Process: How America's Leading Companies Improve Quality*. New York: McGraw-Hill, 1987.

———. *Business Process Improvement: The Breakthrough Strategy for Total Quality, Productivity and Competitiveness*. New York: McGraw-Hill, 1991.

Heifetz, Ronald A. *Leadership Without Easy Answers*. Cambridge, Mass.: The Belknap Press of Harvard University Press, 1994.

Hiers, Ben, and Gordon Pehrson. *The Mind of the Organization: How Western Organizations Can Sharpen Their Thinking*. Cambridge: Harper and Row, 1982.

Hrebiniak, Lawrence G., and William F. Joyce. *Implementing Strategy*. New York: Macmillan Publishing, 1984.

Jaques, Elliott. *Requisite Organization: The CEO's Guide to Creative Structure and Leadership*. Arlington, Va.: Cason Hall and Company, 1989.

Kami, Michael J. *Trigger Points: How to Make Decisions Three Times Faster, Innovate Smarter, and Beat Your Competition by Ten Percent*. New York: McGraw-Hill, 1988.

Kaplan, Robert S., and David P. Norton, *The Balanced Scorecard: Translating Strategy into Action.* Boston: Harvard Business School Press, 1996.

Katzenbach, Jon R., and Douglas K. Smith. *The Wisdom of Teams: Creating the High Performance Organization*. Boston: Harvard Business School Press, 1993.

Katzenbach, Jon R. *Teams at the Top: Unleashing the Potential of Both Teams and Leaders*. Boston: Harvard Business School Press, 1998.

Koestenbaum, Peter. *Leadership: The Inner Side of Greatness*. San Francisco: Jossey-Bass, 1991.

Kotter, John P. *Leading Change*. Boston: Harvard Business School Press, 1996.

Kuhn, Thomas S. *The Essential Tension: Selected Studies in Scientific Tradition and Change*. Chicago: The University of Chicago Press, 1977.

Labovitz, George, and Victor Rosansky. *The Power of Alignment: How Great Companies Stay Centered and Accomplish Extraordinary Things*. New York: John Wiley and Sons, 1997.

Land, George, and Beth Jarman. *Breakpoint and Beyond: Mastering the Future – Today*. New York: Harper Business, 1992.

Locke, Edwin A., and Associates. *The Essence of Leadership: The Four Keys to Leading Successfully*. New York: Lexington Books, 1991.

Lynch, Dudley, and Paul L. Kordis. *Strategy of the Dolphin: Scoring a Win in a Chaotic World*. New York: Fawcett Columbine, 1988.

Lynch, Richard L., and Kelvin F. Cross. *Measure Up: How to Measure Corporate Performance*. 2nd ed. Cambridge, Mass.: Blackwell Business, 1995.

McNally, David. *Even Eagles Need a Push: Learning to Soar in a Changing World*. New York: Dell Trade, 1990.

Mariotti, John L. *The Shape Shifters: Continuous Change for Competitive Advantage*. New York: Van Nostrand Reinhold, 1997.

Maslow, Abraham H. *Eupsychian Management*. Homewood, Ill.: Irwin, 1965.

Means, Grady, and David Schneider. *Meta-Capitalism: The E-Business Revolution and the Design of 21st Century Companies and Markets*. New York: John Wiley and Sons, 2000.

Melcher, Arlyn J. *Structure and Process of Organizations: A Systems Approach*. Englewood Cliffs, N.J.: Prentice Hall, 1976.

Meyer, Christopher, *Fast Cycle Time: How to Align Purpose, Strategy and Structure for Speed*. New York: Free Press, 1993

———. *Relentless Growth: How Silicon Valley Innovation Strategies Can Work in Your Business*. New York: Free Press, 1998.

Meyer, Marc H., and Alvin P. Lehnerd. *The Power of Product Platforms: Building Value and Cost Leadership*. New York: Free Press, 1997.

Miller, James Grier. *Living Systems*. New York: McGraw-Hill, 1978.

Miller, William C. *The Creative Edge: Fostering Innovation Where You Work*. Reading, Mass.: Addison-Wesley, 1987.

Noori, Hamid. *Managing the Dynamics of New Technology: Issues in Manufacturing Management*. Englewood Cliffs, N.J.: Prentice Hall, 1990.

Normann, Richard. *Service Management: Strategy and Leadership in Service Businesses*. Chichester, England: John Wiley and Sons, 1984.

Pascale, Richard Tanner. *Managing on the Edge: How the Smartest Companies Use Conflict to Stay Ahead*. New York: Simon & Schuster, 1990.

Pande, Peter S., Robert P. Neuman, and Roland R. Cavanagh. *The Six Sigma Way: How GE, Motorola, and Other Top Companies Are Honing Their Performance*. New York: McGraw-Hill, 2000.

Penrose, Edith. *The Theory of the Growth of the Firm*. 3rd ed. Oxford, England: Oxford University Press, 1995.

Pfeffer, Jeffrey. *Power in Organizations*. Marshfield, Mass.: Pitman, 1981.

———. *Organizations and Organization Theory*. Boston: Pitman, 1982.

———. *Competitive Advantage Through People: Unleashing the Power of the Workforce*. Boston: Harvard Business School Press, 1994.

Pfeffer, Jeffrey, and Gerald R. Salancik, *The External Control of Organizations: A Resource Dependence Perspective*. New York: Harper and Row, 1978.

Popper, Karl R. *Objective Knowledge: An Evolutionary Approach*. rev. ed. Oxford, England: Oxford University Press, 1979.

Porter, Michael E. *Competitive Strategy: Techniques for Analyzing Industries and Competitors*. New York: Free Press, 1980.

———. "What Is Strategy?" *Harvard Business Review* 74, no. 6 (November–December 1996): 61–78.

Rappaport, Alfred. *Creating Shareholder Value: A Guide for Managers and Investors Revised and Updated*. New York: Free Press, 1998.

Richardson, Peter R. *Cost Containment: The Ultimate Advantage*. New York: Free Press, 1988.

Robson, George D. *Continuous Process Improvement: Simplifying Work Flow Systems*. New York: Free Press, 1991.

Rothschild, William E. *Putting It All Together: A Guide to Strategic Thinking*. New York: Amacom, 1976.

Rummler, Geary A., and Alan P. Brache. *Improving Performance: How to Manage the White Space on the Organization Chart*. 2nd ed. San Francisco: Jossey-Bass, 1995.

Schaffer, Robert H. *The Breakthrough Strategy: Using Short Term Success to Build the High Performance Organization*. New York: Harper Business, 1988.

Schonberger, Richard H. *Building a Chain of Customers: Linking Functions to Create the World Class Company*. New York: Free Press, 1990.

Schwartz, Peter. *The Art of the Long View: Planning for the Future in an Uncertain World*. New York: Currency/Doubleday, 1996.

Senge, Peter M. *The Fifth Discipline: The Art and Practice of the Learning Organization*. New York: Currency/Doubleday, 1990.

Shank, John K., and Vijay Govindarajan. *Strategic Cost Management: The New Tool for Competitive Advantage*. New York: Free Press, 1993.

Sherman, Harvey. *It All Depends: A Pragmatic Approach to Organization*. Tuscaloosa, Ala.: University of Alabama Press, 1966.

Shoemaker, Fred, with Pete Shoemaker. *Extraordinary Golf: The Art of the Possible*. New York: G. P. Putnam's Sons, 1996.

Simons, Robert. *Levers of Control: How Managers Use Innovative Control Systems to Drive Strategic Renewal*. Boston: Harvard Business School Press, 1995.

Skinner, Wickham. *Manufacturing: The Formidable Competitive Weapon*. New York: John Wiley and Sons, 1985.

Slywotzky, Adrian J. *Value Migration: How to Think Several Moves Ahead of the Competition*. Boston: Harvard Business School Press, 1996.

Slywotzky, Adrian J., and David J. Morrison. *The Profit Zone: How Strategic Business Design Will Lead You to Tomorrow's Profits*. New York: Times Business, 1997.

Smith, Theodore A. *Dynamic Business Strategy: The Art of Planning for Success*. New York: McGraw-Hill, 1977.

Stalk, George, Jr., and Thomas M. Hout. *Competing Against Time: How Time-Based Competition Is Reshaping Global Markets*. New York: Free Press, 1990.

Stewart, G. Bennett. *The Quest for Value: The EVA Management Guide*. New York: HarperCollins, 1991.

Thomas, Philip R., with Kenneth R. Martin. *Competitiveness Through Total Cycle Time: An Overview for CEOs.* New York: McGraw-Hill, 1990.

————. *Survival At Nodulex: The Time Based Route to Quality.* Dallas, Tex.: Heritage Publishing, 1994.

Tomasko, Robert M. *Downsizing: Reshaping the Corporation for the Future.* New York: Amacom, 1987.

Twiss, Brian. *Managing Technological Innovation.* 2nd ed. London: Longman, 1980.

Wanniski, Jude. *The Way the World Works.* New York: Touchstone—Simon & Schuster, 1978.

Weisbord, Marvin R. *Discovering Common Ground: How Future Search Conferences Bring People Together to Achieve Breakthrough Innovation, Empowerment, Shared Vision, and Collaborative Action.* San Francisco: Berrett-Koehler, 1992.

Wheelwright, Steven C., and Kim B. Clark. *Revolutionizing Product Development: Quantum Leaps in Speed, Efficiency and Quality.* New York: Free Press, 1992.

Whiteley, Richard C. *The Customer Driven Company: Moving from Talk to Action.* Reading, Mass.: Addison-Wesley, 1991.

Williamson, Oliver E. *Markets and Hierarchies: Analysis and Antitrust Implications.* New York: Free Press, 1975.

Womack, James P., and Daniel T. Jones. *Lean Thinking: Banish Waste and Create Wealth . in Your Corporation.* New York: Simon & Schuster, 1996.

Index

ABOUT THE AUTHORS

WILLIAM R. BIGLER, JR., is President and Founder of S10 Technologies and the Strategy Execution Institute.

MARILYN NORRIS is Founder and Principal of 21st Century Resources.